WHAT READERS ARE SAYING:

Pastor Paul Hatfield captures the heart of Generosity in this must-read book. I believe that similar to contentment, generosity is a learned attribute. Wherever the reader is in his current journey of generosity he is sure to be challenged and encouraged as he encounters the timeless Biblical wisdom incorporated within these pages. The Joy of Generosity is within reach for every believer!

Randall Sanada, CFP, ChFC, MSFS

Kingdom Advisors, Founding Member

Christian Foundation of the West, Chairman

"There is definitely a revolution taking place and Paul Hatfield has nailed it! Generosity and radical living are taking on a new meaning. It's never too late to begin this journey. Hold on for the ride. It's going to be wild and it's going to be great. You just might change your world as God takes you on an adventure you will never regret."

Kenny Sacht, Founder, Wipe Every Tear

If we are honest, I think we'd all admit we are not as generous as we would like to be - or as much as we might sometimes think of ourselves being. My friend Paul does a great job at guiding us through scripture and causing us to think accurately about what being a generous person practically looks like. *Generosity Revolution* is a much needed tool for the Church today.

Chuck Bomar, author of *Better Off Without Jesus* and *Losing Your Religion*

"The Generosity Revolution is a quality book on how to manage finances. It's warm, practical, biblical, and it's filled with illustrations. It's also convicting and would be an excellent resource to share with believers."

Ed Lewis

CE National—

A Church Effectiveness ministry especially connected with Grace Brethren churches

"The ten steps to become a part of the Generosity Revolution are simple, yet we balk at many of them, hesitating to better manage our resources. Pastor Hatfield uses an excellent balance of scripture and personal testimony to successfully make the case that The Generosity Revolution starts with us. No one can read this book and have their life remain the same. Read it, re-read it, and live it – The Generosity Revolution will change the world and it starts with you."

Ben and Sidney McDonald

Co-Authors

The Leadership Compass: Mapping Your Leadership Direction

As a pastor I am always looking for resources that will help people engage with biblical solutions to culturally current issues they are facing in their life. Perhaps there is no more looming issue facing the 21st century Church and Christians than the management of the treasure in which we have been entrusted. For a people who have been placed in the world, but instructed to not be of the world, compounded by the fact that Jesus pointedly said, "For where your treasure is, there your heart will be also." the reality that the Church and Christians are statistically financially no different from the culture should send alarm bells rings throughout Christendom. Pastor Paul, does a masterful job weaving captivating illustrations, biblical truth, and practical application for a Christian wanting to live out the vision God has for them financially.

Dr. Mark McNees

Lead Pastor Element3 Church; Author of

-*Immersion: Live the Life God Envisioned for You*

-*The Six Symbols of the Gospel: Unlocking God's Timeless Truth (Available January 2014)*

The Generosity Revolution is an invitation into a journey that is surprising, inspiring and thoroughly practical. Through biblical principle and real life experience, Paul presents an up-close and personal look at the gift of giving. I highly recommend this book."

Stephan Bauman

President & CEO, World Relief

Sometimes we just need a wake up call to remind us that we are investors in a different kingdom. Being one of the co-founders of Forgo, this is something we are very passionate about. Thanks Paul for reminding us and showing us more ways we can be generous.

Scott Pentzer Co-Founder and President; Forgo.it

Imagine what freedom and fullness in your financial walk with God would mean to you and your loved ones. In Paul Hatfield's new book, Generosity Revolution, you get a step by step roadmap that brings a fresh biblical view on how to look at your finances, to develop a mindset of a responsible faithful giver and to begin the journey leading to financial freedom and fullness for you and your family. I love the simple instructions on how to "round down and round up"... teach this to your family and watch how easy it is to get in step with God's calling to us all. While its never too late to begin this journey, I wish I had this easy to read book in my life decades ago.

Thomas Gay, CEO, 22Touch

THE GENEROSITY REVOLUTION

THE
GENEROSITY
REVOLUTION

Paul Hatfield

endurancepress

The Generosity Revolution is available at special quantity discounts for bulk purchase for sales promotions, premiums, fund-raising, and educational needs. For details write Endurance Press, 577 N Cardigan Ave Star, ID 83669.

Visit Endurance Press' website at www.endurancepress.com

The Generosity Revolution
PUBLISHED BY ENDURANCE PRESS
577 N Cardigan Ave Star, ID 83669 U.S.A.

"Scripture quotations taken from the New American Standard Bible®, Copyright © 1960, 1962, 1963, 1968, 1971, 1972, 1973, 1975, 1977, 1995 by The Lockman Foundation Used by permission." (www.Lockman.org)
italics in Scripture quotations reflects the authors' added emphasis.

Cover photo Teal Rose Design Studios

ISBN 978-0-9856746-9-4

Cover Design by Teal Rose Design Studios
Cover Photo used by permission Teal Rose Design Studios
Author photo courtesy of CKG Photography.

Printed in the United States of America

First Edition 2013

Contents

Introduction 15

Tethered 25

Switch Places with God 35

Plan and Track Your Spending 51

Avoid Consumer Debt 69

Save Intentionally 85

Use Cash Whenever Possible 101

Round Down when Spending and round Up when Giving 111

Make it Automatic 127

Change How You Pray 141

Step it Up 155

Trust Jesus 171

Conclusion 183

Is it ever okay to spend money on myself? 191

Parenting and The Generosity Revolution 199

"I will do whatever it takes
to be as
generous as possible
with the money
that God has entrusted to me."

INTRODUCTION

"I will do whatever it takes to be as generous as possible with the money that God has entrusted to me."

That is the commitment made by those who are a part of The Generosity Revolution. Would you be speaking the truth if you made that statement about yourself right now? Are you that devoted to generosity? It would not surprise me if you are not — *yet*. But imagine with me how different your life would be if you were able to say that someday. Think of what a difference you could make in the lives of those around you. What if you became one of "those" radically generous people that you've heard about and respect so much? Maybe that day can come sooner than you think.

I know what some of you are thinking. "Not me. I don't have the kind of resources to make a difference. My income is too low and my bills are too high." But you can still be a part of this Revolution. The great thing about generosity is that it is not just for rich people to enjoy. Every one of us can be generous. But even those of us with the smallest income can enjoy the eternal joy that is brought by generosity. Ginormous houses, luxurious vacation homes, and fancy sports cars may be reserved exclusively for the wealthy, but generosity is within the reach of everyone. You can be generous with what you have. It isn't the amount that we give that determines the level of generosity, but the percentage that we give and how much of a sacrifice it is for us as individuals. In fact, some of the most generous people on the planet may be those who give very little in actual dollars. Whoever you are, wherever you live, and no matter how much (or how little) money you have, The Generosity Revolution is open to you.

Does this have to be a Revolution? Isn't that a little extreme? Can't we just tweak things a little bit? Not a chance. This has to be a Revolution. Why? Webster's defines a revolution as "an overthrow or repudiation and the thorough replacement of an established government or political system by the people governed." We are held captive and constantly oppressed by a consumer-driven culture that drives us to focus on our own gratification now at the expense of others who spiritually and physically need us to get involved. With so much need and opportunity around us, we can no longer sit back and let things continue the way that they are. We are missing out on the immediate opportunity to make a difference with our lives and are passing up the long-term opportunity to store up eternal rewards that come with living a generous life.

We need a change. Deep inside we know this life of chasing after stuff is not the life that God designed us to live, but maybe you have felt like it is just too late for us. That we are lost, past the point of hope. Let me assure you of something. It is not too late for us. It is not too late for you. A story that has always been of great encouragement to me is found in Acts 3. There is a man who was born with the inability to walk who spent his life trapped by this disability. Every day he went to the gate of the temple in order to beg for any contribution from those who would walk by. He would have never expected his life to change this day, but he was healed of his affliction by the power of Jesus Christ. The statement that encourages me the most about his healing is found in Acts 4:22 where we learn that he had been hindered by his condition for more than forty years. It does not matter how long you have been struggling, how deeply a habit has been ingrained, God can still heal your heart and help you develop new habits of generosity.

When I first presented this material in a sermon series at The Pursuit (www.thepursuit.org), the church where I serve as the Lead Pastor, I challenged our church family to not sit and wait for someone else to do something. A Revolution never begins with everyone waiting for someone else to take the first step. It starts when an individual, or a small pocket of people decide, "Enough is enough; *I* have got to do something—now." A revolution can start anywhere with just one person. I can tell you that The Generosity Revolution has already started in Boise and the rest of the Treasure Valley in Idaho and has begun to spread throughout the U.S. through facebook and our website www.thegenerosityrevolution.

com. I want to invite you personally to begin this adventure of viewing generosity in a totally different way.

If you are a Christian, I am going to assume that you want to be more generous. How can I make that assumption? Because most followers of Jesus I speak with on the topic of generosity say that they want to give more. It is likely that you already want to give when you see God moving in an unique way or when you find someone in desperate need. But many of us have never established the habit of giving. You have only read or heard that you are called be generous, but you have never received practical tips on how to actually give more and therefore have never been able experience the joy of contributing significantly to something that is changing peoples' lives.

I believe most of us want to be known as generous people, but we can't seem to turn the corner. Why? Because we don't know how to manage our money. We have a heart that wants to give, but we don't have the right habits that allow us to give as generously as we want to. I believe we need new habits with our money. Don't misunderstand me. I am not just talking about a giving habit. It is about establishing good habits and making the best choices every time we interact with money.

One of our key problems with falling short in the area of generosity is that most of us think about generosity only on Sundays when the offering is passed. People who are a part of a revolution don't think about their cause once a week. They don't think about their cause on occasion; they are consumed by it. They can't stop thinking about it. When someone goes through a revolution in their approach to eating, moving from a meat-eating diet to a vegetarian or vegan diet, how often do they think about the content of what they eat? Every time they are about to eat, don't they? Such a revolution in how one eats requires constant focus, especially until new actions become natural habits. I have never heard a vegan say, "Oops I forgot I was a vegan and accidentally ate a burger!" I am guessing you have never heard of that either.

For this Generosity Revolution to take place in each of us, generosity is something that we have to start thinking about all of the time until eventually shaping our finances around generosity becomes our new habit. Why? Because the opportunities to spend money are always presenting themselves. Here is a simple truth for all of us. If we spend it, we can't give it. I know it seems obvious when you read it, but have you ever really thought on that? We have to spend less if we are going to give more. And that is what The Generosity Revolution is primarily about.

Generosity is not just about having a heart to give; it is about establishing the right habits with money. What prevents you from being more generous? Are you less generous than you were created to be because you don't have the right heart? Or is it because you lack the right habits? Or maybe, as it is for so many of us, it is a little of both? For those of us who have a heart for God and His ways, we need to change our habits so that we can live on less. When we start to spend less, more will be available to give away as God leads us. This book can move you from being one of those people who wishes they were more generous to actually becoming someone who is radically generous.

I want to come alongside of you on your journey to becoming as generous as you really want to be. Maybe I should say it a little stronger than that. I want to urge you to join The Generosity Revolution. The truth is, I am less concerned about a revolution in society at this point than I am praying for a revolution in each of us individually. This revolution needs to happen in us, not primarily because of what we can do *through* generosity, but because of what generosity can do *in* us. As followers of Jesus in our American culture, our hearts are too divided. Jesus said the greatest commandment (quoting from the Old Testament book of Deuteronomy) is to love God with all of our heart, not part of it. Look at Mark 12:30. "And you shall love the Lord your God with *all* your heart, and with *all* your soul, and with *all* your mind, and with *all* your strength" (NASB, emphasis mine). As the Psalmist writes in Psalm 86:11, my prayer is that God would give us an undivided heart. He rightfully deserves our whole heart. What does this have to do with our hearts?

Jesus taught that what we do with our money impacts our heart for Him. God definitely desires for you and me as individuals to be generous; we are made to give. But He does not want us to be generous for His sake. You know that He doesn't need our help, right? He wants to help us experience true life. God wants us to be generous because He cares about our hearts. I heard Steven Furtick, pastor of Elevation Church in Charlotte, North Carolina (www.elevationchurch.org), say it this way: "God doesn't want generosity from you; He wants generosity for you." With what is at stake in us and around us, we need this Generosity Revolution.

Now, I am sure there are probably some of you who for whatever reason are not excited about learning how to be more generous and are possibly ready to stop reading. Maybe you aren't really sure about following Jesus at all but somehow this book ended up in your hands. If you are not necessarily excited to give more, whatever your reason may be, you can just substitute whatever financial goal you have instead of giving, and this book will help you accomplish that goal. Is it starting to save? Getting a new car? Paying for your kids' college (or paying off your college debt)? Unless your goal is to spend everything that comes in as quickly as possible (which is not advised, although it seems to be the goal of most Americans), this book is going to be a blessing to you.

For those of you who are not yet followers of Jesus, I would strongly encourage you to consider God's way of handling money. You've tried doing what everyone else is doing. How's that working for you? Look around. How is it working for everyone else? Doing what everyone else is doing is not working as our continued economic challenges and stresses prove. Why not try something else?

I want to challenge you to try an experiment. Why not take Jesus's advice? The Bible was written over a 1500 year time period and was completed nearly 2000 years ago, and yet it is unbelievably practical today and there is no better area in which to apply the teachings of the Bible than in the area of finances. Perhaps if you trust God by beginning to follow Him in the area of finances, you will realize that He is trustworthy in all things and you will end up giving Him full leadership of your life. Will you consider it?

So let's get into it. I am going to give you ten steps, one per chapter, that you can do that will allow you to be more generous than you have thought possible. You are not necessarily going to be able to do all of these fully right away. Some of them are somewhat philosophical, and it will take some time to change the way that you think and react. But there are also some that are extremely practical which you can start implementing them into your life immediately. Applying these ten steps is how The Generosity Revolution can start with you.

So are you ready? Before we dive in, I just want to say clearly that although this book is about establishing good habits with our money, it really is not actually primarily about money. It is not about behavior. It is about our hearts for God that can be so easily pulled away from Him by the things of the world. I believe that God can do a great work in our hearts as we read and apply the principles in this book to our finances. Because the heart is of utmost importance, before we get into the ten steps, I want to spend one chapter addressing the heart. In addition, to maintain the focus on our heart throughout the book, I have included a "Heart Check" at the end of each of the ten steps.

It is my prayer that God will reveal to each one of us where our habits need to be modified and where our hearts need to change. It is my hope that through this journey, you personally would be able to say, "I will do whatever it takes to be as generous as possible with the money God has entrusted to me. I am a part of The Generosity Revolution."

Chapter 1

TETHERED

Imagine if you went to do a physical and your doctor was concerned that there might be a heart issue, so he sent you to a heart specialist who was well-known for her ability to diagnose issues of the heart. After a conversation with her, she also became immediately concerned based on the symptoms you described, so she put you through a stress test on a treadmill and then ran an Echo cardiogram and an MRI. If, after these tests, she sat with you in her office and presented the evidence and explained that she thought you had an issue with your heart, what would you do? Would you be interested in what she had to say? Would you listen?

Who is the expert on diagnosing a spiritual heart issue? Jesus is, right? He made us. He knows our hearts and what can strengthen or destroy them. What if many of us who attend church and do other things that make us look spiritually "healthy" actually have a serious spiritual heart issue, or at least one that is developing? This chapter may be difficult to read just as it would be difficult to hear bad news after a physical diagnosis, but there is hope because there is a clear path for healing. It is found in the word of God. We have a choice every time we hear the word, to soften our heart or harden it. My prayer for you as you read this is that you would be willing to listen to what God may have to say to you about your heart.

First off, I do not believe that we modern, westerners are intentionally selfish people. We simply struggle with the issue of surrender of our finances. "What is the big deal? So I don't handle money well. Maybe it is just a habit issue?" The problem is, even if it starts out as a habit-issue, it will become a heart issue over time. Jesus said something incredibly alarming. He encouraged people to give money away to things that would honor God and then explains why. "For where your treasure is, there your heart will be also" (Luke 12:34). Although it is true that what we do with our money today reveals where our heart is today, that is not Jesus's point.

It is much bigger than that. He is saying that where we put our money actually is more of an indicator of where our hearts will be — it shows where our hearts are headed. We could talk about many sins that reflect where our heart is currently, but money is unique. Jesus said how we spend our money is the key indicator of where our hearts are going to be.

It is incredibly dangerous for our hearts tomorrow to not deal right with our money today. Our hearts are irresistibly pulled to wherever our money goes. We can't help it. For many of us Christians today, for far too long, too much of our treasure has been going to this world — and our hearts have been following it. For some of us, our hearts are being led away and we need to make minor corrections. For others of us, the build up over the years requires some drastic intervention. We need to resolve the money issue right now for our heart's sake.

If you are not prioritizing your finances biblically, I can promise you that God views this as an urgent matter. The money issue is so significant to God that He wants it resolved in us the moment we come to faith in Jesus, even though for many of us it was not.

Why would this be so important to God as a first thing? Because He's a little down on His luck and needs a hand out? No. He's doing quite well for Himself! Because He knows the pull that money has on our hearts, and He wants to protect our commitment to Him.

In Luke 3, three different groups asked John the Baptist what they should start doing to show that they had made a commitment to God. His reply to all three dealt with how they interacted with money. Read this carefully and then we'll talk about it.

And the crowds were questioning him, saying, "Then what shall we do?" And he would answer and say to them, "The man who has two tunics is to share with him who has none; and he who has food is to do likewise." And some tax collectors also came to be baptized, and they said to him, "Teacher, what shall we do?" And he said to them, "Collect no more than what you have been ordered to." Some soldiers were questioning him, saying, "And what about us, what shall we do?" And he said to them, "Do not take money from anyone by force, or accuse anyone falsely, and be content with your wages." - Luke 3:10-14.

He could have said anything to these three groups of people, but what did he say? To the first group, he said, "Handle your possessions, your 'extra,' differently. Take some of what you have, and give it away." To the next group, the tax collectors, he said, "Handle your money differently. Stop stealing. Stop taking advantage of people because you want more money." It is about money again. And then to the soldiers? "You have a heart issue that centers around money. Be content with what you have. Stop stealing too." He adds not accusing anyone falsely, which at first glance may not seem like it deals with money, although frequently people were bribed to accuse someone, so it was likely a money issue after all.

Three different groups of people ask what they should do first as they begin their walk with God. He could have told these three groups anything. "You need to pray more. Love your kids better. Study the scriptures. Be kind. Stop getting drunk. Live with sexual purity." Those are the things we tell people when they become Christians today, and we should not neglect calling them to do so. But he didn't suggest those things. What did he tell them? "Handle your money and possessions differently." Why? Because where your treasure is, there your heart will be also. Because your heart will be pulled away from God by the power of money and possessions. There is no scriptural support for the western phenomenon of allowing God into our finances much later in our journey of following Jesus. It is safe to say that we aren't completely surrendered to God if we haven't completely surrendered our finances.

So what about you? I want you to think back to when you first decided to follow Jesus. Did how you handle your money change drastically at that point? There is a good possibility that it didn't, and that is largely the fault of those who were leading you at the time. They didn't tell you that you needed to for your sake, did they? They were probably afraid that you would think they were after your money so they held off on this important teaching. Honestly, they probably didn't fully understand how important giving was either.

It really would not be surprising if there has been little change to how you use money even if you've been a Christian for years. The truth is, most Christians are hardly more generous than people who profess no faith in Jesus. Most have the same debt loads and live paycheck to paycheck just like everyone else.

I think Satan has been tricking us, blinding us to how important this is. Why would he do that? Because if you didn't start giving back then, your heart for God has continued to be tethered to the world. In fact, it may explain why you have not grown more on fire for God over time. So many Christians I know seem to be less excited about Jesus and impacting the world around them than they were at the beginning of their walks with Him. Has your spiritual trajectory been flatter than you'd hoped? If you struggle to have your heart in so much of what He's called you to do, maybe this is why. It is because your heart is tethered. Rather than becoming more and more devoted to Jesus, because of your money choices, your heart has become more and more tethered to the world.

Jesus met a man named Zaccheus. He was short. He was a wee little man actually, as the old kids' song goes. Because he was vertically challenged, he climbed up into a tree so that he could see Jesus as he passed by. Jesus engages this man, and Zaccheus gave his life to Jesus through their interaction. Look at what this man, a rich tax-collector (who certainly would have collected more than was required of him), said upon his conversion to Jesus. "Zaccheus stopped and said to the Lord, 'Behold, Lord, half of my possessions I will give to the poor, and if I have defrauded anyone of anything, I will give back four times as much'" (Luke 19:8). Unprompted, he decided to give away half of what he had. Half! Yes, he was rich, but that would be half of a lot, so he gave away a lot. And he committed to make restitution for any wrong he had done financially by paying back those whom he had offended — four times as much. Incredible!

Jesus thought it was pretty radical too. Look at Jesus's response. "And Jesus said to him, 'Today salvation has come to this house'" (Luke 19:9). I want to be clear: Jesus isn't saying that Zaccheus was saved because he decided to give, but rather that there was such a drastic turning away from his own riches that it was evident that he was genuinely repentant of his sins.

Is it possible for you to be genuinely saved and not handle your money differently? One thing we can definitely say from the Bible. If you do not handle your money differently, it is not possible for your heart to be fully set aside for God. Our hearts have been tethered for too long. Something has to change in us so things can change around us.

What are the true consequences when our hearts are tethered? The condition of our heart does not just impact us, but it directly impacts those closest to us. We know that sins in our heart impact other people in other areas. If you have anger in your heart, does it impact the people closest to you? Absolutely. If you have insecurity in your heart, does it impact the people closest to you? You bet it does. Our heart being tethered to the world impacts those closest to us as well. It would not surprise me if some of you are suffering financially because you have not been honoring God with your finances.

You may have heard people say, "If God wants us to have it, He will give it to us." That sounds spiritual, but it is incredibly unbiblical. God wanted to give Israel the promised land but didn't do so right away because of their disobedience. If you are one of God's children, He loves you too much to reward disobedience. If you have a small child and you tell them to come to you, and they don't, do you go give them a piece of candy and praise them for their disobedience? Of course not. Neither does God. Is it possible that you are facing financial difficulties that are directly the result of failing to give back to God, of putting all of your treasures into earthly things? I know that some of you are in a season of struggling financially even though you've been faithful, so I am not saying that everyone who is struggling is being disobedient. But the Bible is very clear that God will give to those who give to Him and He withholds from those who don't. Failing to give doesn't just tether our hearts, we can end up with finances that are tethered. He will not let some of you get out of the financial mess you are in without inviting Him into the situation by starting to give.

In Malachi 3, God explains to the people of Israel that He is withholding financial blessing because of their misuse of their resources. He actually tells them they are cursed! What does God tell them? "Bring the whole tithe into the storehouse, so that there may be food in My house" (Malachi 3:10a). We'll talk more about the tithe later, but for now let's just say he tells them to bring all that they were called to give. We need to understand the ramifications of our financial choices. When our hearts are tethered because we spend all of our money on earthly things, it isn't just ministries and churches that are tethered; our families are tethered too.

If you are financially struggling and have not been giving generously to God, then you can't afford to wait until things turn around. God wants you to trust Him, and He wants to help you. He wants to protect your heart.

Do you know what excites me about The Generosity Revolution? It is not just that our churches and ministries no longer being financially tethered; it is that our hearts will no longer be tethered. If where are our treasure is, there our hearts will be also, then as we surrender our finances to God and contribute more to His work, our hearts are going to be pulled towards God in every area It is not just our finances that will be different. Our marriages will be different. Our families will be different. We're going to turn from sexual sin We're going to overcome other sins because our hearts will finally be pulled towards God by how we utilize the money with which we've been entrusted.

Where is your heart being pulled? Answer this question honestly: Am I investing primarily in eternity? Just like overeating can lead to physical heart disease, overspending can lead to spiritual heart disease. It can tether our hearts. It is time for a change. So are you ready? Let's look at the ten steps that you can take to be a part of The Generosity Revolution

Chapter Two

STEP I

SWITCH PLACES WITH GOD

In our home, as our kids began to speak, they started to speak some words that required our immediate attention. One word that we had to deal with was the word "no." I can remember exactly where I was sitting and where our first daughter, Meghan, was standing the first time she said that to me. I thought, "Where did that come from? Who taught her that?" Stubbornness certainly shows up early in our development.

But the second word that required our immediate correction is the one I want to focus on with you. It was the word "MINE." Does that surprise you? I don't know why any parent who takes their role in training up their children in the ways of our God would let their children say "mine" without correcting it immediately. "Mine" is a four letter word in our house. I guess it is in your house too, but you know what I mean!

Whenever one of our children would say the word "mine," we would jump in immediately. "It is not yours; it is God's," we would explain to them. "You are simply to take care of it." Even today, as our children are growing older, when the word "mine" occasionally slips out of one of their mouths, it is followed up with, "Whose is it?" "God's" they answer.

Why did we decide to make such a big deal of this from the beginning? Because as soon as they began to understand what possessing something meant, we wanted them to understand that they don't actually possess anything. We wanted them to know that they didn't own anything.

I don't either, and neither do you. Everything belongs to God. God says to the people of Israel in Haggai 2:8, " 'The silver is Mine and the gold is Mine,' declares the LORD of hosts." The money we possess is not actually in our possession. God possesses it. It is His. He never actually signed over ownership of any of it when He placed it under our care. And God's ownership isn't limited to our money and possessions, but extends to everything and everyone that is in the world. Psalm 24:1 says, "The earth is the LORD'S, and all it contains, the world, and those who dwell in it." We belong to God. For those of us who are parents, even our children belong to God. They are under our care, but they do not belong to us.

This is true, by the way, whether you are a follower of Jesus yet or not. You belong to God. The difference between a follower of Jesus and one that isn't yet is that those of us who are followers have acknowledged this truth and surrendered everything to God. We willingly give our lives to Jesus because He is the rightful owner. He is the Master.

The apostle Paul, in His exhortation to flee sexual immorality in 1 Corinthians 6, closes out his thoughts with a reminder that we really don't have the freedom to take our body, which is no longer ours, and do with it what we please. He spells it out clearly for us when he tells them and us: "Do you not know that your body is a temple of the Holy Spirit who is in you, whom you have from God, and that you are not your own? For you have been bought with a price: therefore glorify God in your body" (1 Corinthians 6:19-20).

As a Christian, we are to acknowledge that we belong to God. But somehow, Satan our enemy has tricked us Americans into believing that we can surrender ourselves to God but still maintain our finances as if they are our own. But Jesus makes it clear that we are to surrender everything, including our money and possessions, in order to become His child.

Jesus said, "So then, none of you can be My disciple who does not give up all his own possessions" (Luke 14:33). It could not be any more clear. We are not going to be able to truly follow Jesus unless we give up all of our possessions. Why? Our stuff will have a hold over us if we hold on to it. As we discussed in the last chapter, our hearts will be pulled away. There has been a lot of conversation about becoming a disciple, not just a "convert" lately. Although I understand and appreciate that we are called to be followers who are seeking after Jesus, this distinction has allowed some to believe that they can become a convert without being a disciple, as if becoming a disciple is something we eventually become as we mature. But this distinction is not a biblical concept. "Disciple" which means 'follower' is the word used to describe "converts" or "Christians" in the gospels.

Jesus is saying that surrendering ourselves (and our money and everything else) is part of coming to faith in Him. Those aren't my words; those are Jesus's. When those of us who are followers of Jesus are baptized, we take out our wallet and keys so they won't get wet. We make sure that we don't take any valuables into the water with us. Unfortunately, I think for some of us, that was symbolic. We never really turned it all over to God. I think that maybe American churches should start bringing ziploc baggies for when people are baptized so that they can take their wallet in with them! Everything must be surrendered to Him.

I think sometimes we choose to believe our view of reality over what Jesus said was reality. It is amazing how easily Christians deceive themselves. In Luke 18, Jesus tells a young man that he must sell everything he has and give it to the poor, because that would get in the way of his heart. He said to him, "You'll have treasure in heaven. Come and follow me."

It says that the young man went away sad. He couldn't do it. I have heard many Christians say, "I would have given up everything to follow Him. How crazy of him to choose earthly riches over following Jesus!"

Let me ask you though: What would you have done, really? Can I ask you a hard question? If you aren't giving even 10% to Him now, which has been histor-ically considered the baseline of giving, what makes you so sure you'd really give 100% if He asked? I'd say the prospects aren't very good.

It is so easy to deceive ourselves. It is much easier to talk about making the ultimate sacrifice than it is to actually make a sacrifice of so much less. It is like we husbands who say we would take a bullet for our wives, but then somehow we can't handle dishpan hands. "It hurts my lower back, honey, because the sink is so low. It's not built for big men like me." Yeah, I used to use that line too.

Jesus does call us to give up all of our possessions, to surrender everything to Him. When we get our pay-check, we should imagine that it is made out to us and Jesus. It is all His, not just the percentage we intend to give. "What do I want to do with my money?" is a question I should never ask, because I don't have any money. "What does God want me to do with His money?" is the question I need to ask.

So where does that leave us if it all belongs to Him? We just manage some of His money. We are called to be investors, not consumers. Think about that for a second. Who labeled us consumers? Is it in the Bible somewhere? There is no verse in the Bible that says, "Spend! Spend! Spend! Get all you can!" What does Jesus say to us? Picture Him handing you some of His money to manage and giving you this instruction on what to do with it:

"Do not store up for yourselves treasures on earth, where moth and rust destroy, and where thieves break in and steal. But store up for yourselves treasures in heaven, where neither moth nor rust destroys, and where thieves do not break in or steal; for where your treasure is, there your heart will be also." - Matthew 6:19-21

Do you understand what He is saying? He is telling us that the reason He is transferring a portion of His money under our care is that He want us to be investors. He could not be any clearer in His intentions. Money comes with instructions. We are not called to be consumers, but rather to be investors — investors in eternity. Can you imagine how differently you would handle money if you started to view your main purpose for receiving income as investing it wisely in line with God's priorities? How different would your financial picture look? If our money isn't ours but instead belongs to God, and He gives it to us along with instructions to invest in heaven with it, not just consume earthly goods, perhaps it is time we make some drastic changes.

When I worked with Francis Chan at Cornerstone Community Church in Simi Valley, I remember him telling a story in a sermon one time about someone in the congregation who had the coolest job of anyone he had ever met. He explained that this person's job was to manage the charitable giving for a multi-billionaire. He shared that this man was given a bunch of money that he was to donate to various charities of his choice.

How cool would it be to have a job like that? But it actually got better. If you can believe this, this person was allowed to keep whatever money he needed to live on out of the money that was given to him with absolute freedom to set his own salary. What a sweet set up! I think everyone in the room was wishing that they had that job. Then Francis dropped the bomb on all of us as he so effectively does. He said that every one of us already had that job! That is exactly what God does with us. (He entrusts us with money, and our time and abilities for that matter) to invest in His work in the world and is so gracious that He lets us keep some of the money on which we are able to live. He doesn't legislate the limits on what we should spend. He trusts us. With this perspective, shouldn't we handle our finances in line with the purpose that God has set for us? We are called to be investors. God is the only owner.

So how would you rate yourself as an investor? As the owner of all things, do you know what God does with His money? He entrusts it to faithful people to manage. Here's a question I would like you to consider: Are you the type of money manager to whom God would want to entrust more of his money? How have you done taking care of what he has entrusted to you so far? If he called you to give an account for what you have done, what would you say?

I am not sure that most of us in our culture should reasonably expect God to entrust us with more in the future. Here's why: If you hired an investor to manage a portion of your money, and then he went blew it all on himself, would you give him any more? Of course not! Then why would we expect God to trust us with more if that is what we have done with what He has given us to this point? Look at the words of Jesus recorded in Luke 16:10-12:

"He who is faithful in a very little thing is faithful also in much; and he who is unrighteous in a very little thing is unrighteous also in much. Therefore if you have not been faithful in the use of unrighteous wealth, who will entrust the true riches to you? And if you have not been faithful in the use of that which is another's, who will give you that which is your own?"

We should strive to be the type of managers to whom God could confidently entrust more, not just of money, but of everything under our management. I don't know if you are in the habit of taking good care of your possessions, but since they are not actually ours, we should take good care of them. Why would God trust us with more if we don't take care of what he has already entrusted to us? It is easy to have the attitude of, "If I had a nicer car, I'd take better care of it." That is not the response of someone who understands God's ownership. Take good care of what God has already entrusted to you and perhaps he will trust you with more and better in the future. Keep the oil changed. Change your filters on your furnace. Keep your gutters clear.

It would be appropriate for me to mention the care of your own body at this point too. It is not your body. It belongs to God. If it was yours, you would have the freedom to not take care of yourself, to "let yourself go." But you were bought with a price. Floss regularly. You should take care of your teeth. They are not your teeth. Exercise regularly. Take care of your heart. It is not your heart. Pay attention to what you eat. The principle of God's ownership and our role as managers impacts everything. We've been given a life to invest. Let's not squander it by slipping into the role of just being a consumer.

Switch places with God. He's the owner. You take the role of investor. When I taught this principle at The Pursuit, we handed out plastic cards that read "Investor" across the top that could slide in front of (not behind) our credit or debit cards in our wallets. That way, whenever we open our wallets, we are reminded that we are called to be investors. You can visit our website at www. thegenerosityrevolution.com where you can print out a PDF version that you can cut out and place in your wallet. We need to think of ourselves as investors. That is the first step. With that as the foundation, we are ready for step number two.

But before we move on, perhaps I should ask: Have you ever really surrendered all of your resources to God? Have you? It is easy to say that you have, but maybe you should draw a line in the sand and make a formal declaration. It was when I took a class from Crown Ministries (www.crown.org), a biblical financial stewardship ministry to whom so many of us are indebted, that I first saw an example of a Quit Claim Deed with which we could mark our surrender of everything to God.

I would encourage you to visit our website where you can download a Quit Claim Deed. Take some time to think of all of the things that are valuable to you — your home, your car, your IRA, your boat or motorcycle, your jewelry, your guitar (you get the idea) — write them down and sign them over to God. And don't limit it to just material things. What else is precious to you? Your spouse, your children, your hobbies and abilities? Remember, He owns it all. Sign everything over to Him.

This can be a very powerful experience if we are sincere. For this to actually take hold in your heart, you are going to actually need to mourn the loss of everything. You are going to have to emotionally release everything. How do you let go of material things that have become too important to you? How can you let go of them while they are still in your possession?

I love what the apostle Paul did. In Philippians 4, Paul speaks of his personal victory in learning to be content. He had lost so much and yet he expressed that he was content when he had plenty and remained content even when he had lost all of his earthly possessions. How was he able to do that? I believe the answer is found in what the apostle Pauls says in Philippians 3:7-8: "But whatever were gains to me I now consider loss for the sake of Christ. What is more, I consider everything a loss because of the surpassing worth of knowing Christ Jesus my Lord, for whose sake I have lost all things. I consider them garbage..."

The reason that Paul was okay with losing everything is that he devalued it (or honestly saw the true value of it) in his own mind ahead of time. Things were no longer precious to him. He considered them "garbage." That word in the Greek actually is best translated "dung." Animal excrement. Manure. I'll never forget the image of Francis Chan carrying around a bag of manure on the stage to illustrate how ridiculous it is for us to boast in our stuff.

Compared to the riches of knowing Christ and the eternal rewards we have in Him, everything on this earth really is dung in comparison. Some of us have the common steer manure. Some of us are blessed to have the expensive chicken manure. But it is all manure. Kind of makes you look at your car a little differently, huh? Some of you drive some really nice manure!

Why did Paul consider everything else dung? So that he could gain Christ. So it wouldn't get in the way of his relationship with God. So his heart would not be tethered. What we let go of on this earth (and we will eventually let go of all of it) is nothing compared to, as Paul writes, the "surpassing worth" of knowing Jesus. By giving up control of everything, you really do have nothing to lose. Nothing that is really worth anything anyways. It is only manure. So could you let go of your money and stuff? Could you surrender it all to Jesus? I'd urge you to stop and do that right now.

Holding onto what is not yours will hinder you from being the generous person you want to be and the fully devoted follower that God has created you to be. Our stuff, and even our own lives, must be set aside for us to live as God has called us to live. The apostle Paul didn't just devalue his stuff. He devalued his own comfort and life. Look at what he says. "However, I consider my life worth nothing to me; my only aim is to finish the race and complete the task the Lord Jesus has given me — the task of testifying to the good news of God's grace" (Acts 20:24). My prayer is that we would all switch places with God. That we would no longer cling to and pursue the things of this world. Would you surrender everything right now?

Heart Check

It is one thing to say we've surrendered everything, but how can we tell if we really have? How can we be certain that in our hearts we have truly acknowledged that He is the owner of everything and we are just his managers? How can we be absolutely sure that we have recognized that our cars are His, our bank accounts are His, and "our" most prized possessions are not really ours?

Perhaps the best way our hearts are tested in regards to surrendering everything is how we respond when something we have surrendered breaks or is taken away from us. It is easy to say that we have surrendered our 401K to God, but how do we respond when the balance goes down.. significantly? Think about it, if the 401K belongs to God, then shouldn't He be the one who gets upset when the value drops? Why would we? It isn't ours.

I remember a couple of years ago when there was a sharp downward trend in housing prices in the Boise area (which is true in most of the country). When assessed values came out every year, I seemed to hear many conversations referencing the sick feeling people got when they saw how much the value of their home has dropped. I felt like interrupting (which I have not had the boldness to do yet) and asking them why it bothers them that God's house dropped in price.

We do know that God is indeed in control of everything in the universe, including our American economy, right? I can't imagine that heaven gets all in knots around the time when assessment statements are mailed. Do you think the angels get a little skittish around the throne? Can you picture the angels concerned that God's personal net worth may go down? Obviously I am being a little ridiculous, but isn't it a little ridiculous that we get bothered over what happens to God's possessions? He is okay with it. Shouldn't we be?

If everything is God's, then why should we get bothered when the car breaks down and we have to spend His money to fix it? It is His car, and He is in control. If you work for a company and drive a company car and it needs repairs, do you get frustrated? Of course not! It is not yours. You don't have to pay for it. The company pays for the repairs. The same is true when your personal car breaks down. It isn't your car. It isn't your money that goes to repair it. You are just taking care of the transaction for God. It is God's money. You basically submit a check request form to God's accounting department and the money comes out of His account, which you happen to manage, to pay for it. You are just managing his resources.

We have a line in our household that others at The Pursuit have started to adopt and I would encourage it to become part of your vocabulary. Whenever there is an unexpected expense or we are forced to spend money we were not wanting to, instead of getting frustrated over "our" loss, we simply say, "If that's how God wants to spend his money, that's okay with me." We have to trust that He is in control and that for some reason (I am guessing to build our character), He wants to use up some of His money in these ways.

I can remember quite vividly driving down our one freeway in Boise shortly after I had my cracked windshield replaced. A truck in front of me dropped a rock and it struck my windshield and put a nice chip in it. My immediate reaction was about to head towards frustration, but my mind went to this teaching. Instead of getting frustrated, I acknowledged (out loud!) that it was God's windshield and if that's how He wanted to take care of it, that was okay with me. Then it hit me. It was also His rock! I asked jokingly out loud, "Why would *You* send *Your* rock into *Your* newly replaced windshield?" How could I really be frustrated after that? I just laughed and eventually had it repaired.

Do you know how freeing it is to no longer get stressed when things break? It is important that we are not negligent and careless, but when we are being faithful stewards, we have no reason to be concerned when we have to use some of God's money on stuff that was not necessarily how we were hoping to spend it.

So, next time something breaks down or something is lost or stolen, remind yourself that it is just manure and that it is not where your hope and identity are found. Maybe you'll need to pull our your Quit Claim Deed to remind yourself that it all belongs to God. And if it helps, just say out loud, "God, if that's how You want to spend Your money, that's okay with me."

Chapter Three

STEP 2

PLAN AND TRACK YOUR SPENDING

"I wish I had more hours in my day." I can't tell you how many times I've heard that. I've even said it myself. If you haven't said it out loud, you've certainly at least thought it. But let me ask you something. Would that really make a difference? Would that really solve all of your busyness problems? Think back to the last time you "gained" an hour of sleep when your clocks fell back to mark the end of daylight savings time. What did you do with that time? Use it for something profitable? If you are like most people with whom I interact, you probably just wasted it. Don't beat yourself up. I'm only trying to make a point.

We live under this delusion that more time is the answer to our busy lives. Honestly, if someone doesn't manage his or her time well, why do we think that having more would solve the problem? Perhaps it would just magnify the problem even further. Our problem is not that we don't have enough time (unless we think God made a mistake when He created the day with only 24 hours in it). The problem is that we don't manage the time that we have properly. We are not going to get more time, so we'd better just get better at managing the time we have.

If you have difficulty in this area, I'd encourage you to read books or attend a seminar on time management. They can give you practical tools that will help you. But you know you don't actually get any more time when you implement the principles you learn. You will have the same amount of hours as before you got these new tools, but suddenly you will feel like you have more. For those of you who don't have the time to take a class or read a book on time management (yes, I am intentionally being ironic here), let me give you one tip you can implement right away that will give you "more time." If you want to have more time, plan what you are going to do with the time you have ahead of time. Decide how you are going to spend your time before you get it to spend and you will end up having more time.

The same principle applies to handling money. Most people think that they just need a little bit more money and then things would be better for them. It doesn't matter what level of income people have, most people say they need more to live comfortably. Not a lot more, but just a little. Maybe 10% or 20% more. In fact, if I were to ask you what it would take for you to be more generous, it would not surprise me if you receiving more income would be one of your top answers.

I think most Christians would say that if their income went up, they would probably give more. I wonder if you've ever had the thought, "I wish I had a lot of money so I could be generous"? It is as if we are thinking, "If God will give me more, than I will give Him more." But think about this for a minute. Did the percentage you gave away go up the last time you had an increase in income? If it did, that is awesome, but you'd be in the minority.

I know there are people with various ranges of income and certainly there are some of you who are reading this who genuinely make less than you need to live comfortably at the moment. Some of us really do need more money to meet our family's needs, sometimes because of poor choices and sometimes because of circumstances outside of our control. But do you know that most of us don't need more money to live and even to give more? We just need to manage what we have better.

It will feel like we have more if we learn to plan and track our spending. As I mentioned in the last chapter, God wants us to be faithful with what He's already given us before He will entrust us with more. God is very good with His money. If you sat down with a financial advisor to whom you were considering entrusting some of your money for retirement or other investments, and he explained to you that he doesn't plan ahead on how to invest your money, would you entrust your money to him? People who have money and are smart with it don't entrust it to people who don't have a plan. Why would God give us more of His money if we have no idea what we are going to do with it? Why would He give you a raise at work if you don't have a good plan for it when it comes? What is your plan for your next paycheck? It is God's money as we have already learned, so we should have a plan for how we are going to use it.

We can look at it this way. If you knew God was going to give you $250K, would you sit down and plan how you were going to spend it? I think most of us would. For most of us, God is going to give us $250K Some of you may earn that in the next 6 mos. For the majority of Americans, it will take several years. In the Boise area where I live, according to the median income, many will earn it in the next 4-5 years. For some of you, it may take ten But God is going to give you some of His money to manage. Shouldn't you decide ahead of time what you are going to do with it?

I want to jump back to those of you who don't have generosity as your top goal. What is your goal? More savings? Pay off debt? Buy an SUV for the family? Go on a cruise? What is your goal? It would be worth coming up with three goals. Once you have those goals established, you need a plan to reach your goal. This is always true. If you had a goal to lose ten pounds but did not take the time to develop a plan to see it accomplished, how likely is it that you'd actually be successful? Not very. Your goals will give you the motivation to have a spending plan.

So let's talk about planning. Now I was very strategic in choosing the word planning instead of budgeting. If I would have said "budgeting," some of you might have pushed back. "Budget" is not a swear word. Budgeting is simply planning. I know that there are some who immediately tremble at the idea of putting together a budget or spending plan. The fear is that it will be too restrictive. That is nonsense. You fill out your own spending plan! You set the limits where they need to be in order for you to accomplish your priorities. If there is not enough allocated to a certain area of spending, make the adjustment. Just make sure it balances at the end and reflects the priorities you are setting out to accomplish.

The Spending Plan produces freedom; it is not restrictive. You are already restricted by the income you currently have, although some choose to ignore those limits to their own financial demise. The Spending Plan simply makes sure that you stay within safe boundaries that you put in place based on your goals. It is for your financial safety. Do you ever feel like you wish you had more freedom to drive however you feel like driving? Wouldn't it be great if you could drive however fast you wanted? On whatever side of the road? How great would it be if you could throw off the restraint of traffic signals and just go when you felt like it? It would be a disaster. Your desire for freedom would quickly get you injured or killed.

We have an authority that has set rules in place to govern the road for our safety and the safety of those around us. You have to come in as the authority and set the rules in place for your finances for your own safety. I heard John Maxwell, the great teacher on leadership, say, "Budgeting (or having a spending plan) is telling your money where it is going to go instead of wondering where it went." Do you ever wonder where your money went? The Good Sense course defines it as the fundamental tool that enables us to control our money so that it doesn't end up controlling us.

Many people who have higher incomes mistakenly believe that budgeting or having a spending plan is only for people with smaller incomes. But having a spending plan is not just about financial survival. It is about being a good investor. It is about the attention of our heart. For those who are a part of The Generosity Revolution, it is about being able to be as generous as possible with the money God has entrusted to us. The more we make, the more diligent we need to be to have a plan. God is trusting some of us with a lot. I guarantee you from personal experience and studies, if we don't plan our spending, we are wasting some of God's money. People with little income can waste a little of God's money. People with a lot can waste a lot. God expects more from those to whom He has entrusted more. "From everyone who has been given much, much will be required" (Luke 12:48). If you aren't budgeting, unless you are an incredible tightwad that never spends anything (you know who you are), you are wasting money.

If you are making a lot of money and are not using a spending plan, you are wasting a lot of God's money. Some of you may feel like you have enough that it is okay that you are wasting some (or a lot). But it is not our money to waste, is it? It belongs to God. How does

He feel about waste? In John 6, Jesus feeds 5000 people with five loaves of bread and two fish. He multiplied food. It is so easy to read that story without stopping to think about how amazing that is. But something interesting happens when he is done. What does Jesus tell the disciples to do afterwards? Gather up all of the remaining food so that none could be wasted. If anyone could have wasted food, it was Jesus. He could have just manifested more! But He didn't want anything to go to waste. You may feel like you can just go get more money so it is okay to waste it, but Jesus does not want what is His going to waste. If you have been given much, there is so much you can do for the kingdom. There is so much need around us! If we want to be more generous, we need to have a plan for the money we manage.

If you go to www.thegenerosityrevolution.com, you can download a PDF version of a Spending Plan adapted from the Good Sense budget course. Fill it out. This may be a lot of work, but you will probably need to go back and look at what you've been spending in order to fill it out.

When you fill out your spending plan, you'll notice the first line item after listing your income is giving. Put God first. It is really a simple order of priority. Give, save, spend. That's the order of those who want to be a part of The Generosity Revolution. How much should you give? As much as possible, right? A question that frequently comes up whenever giving to the church and other ministries is discussed is: "Are New Testament

Christians required to give the tithe (the first 10%) back to God or was that just an Old Testament law for Jews?"

Let's look at that for a moment. There are a few examples of people who tithed in the New Testament, but they were Pharisees, who were Jews and were under the law. And it is really not a great example of righteousness because in Luke 16:14 it says that the Pharisees were lovers of money, which means they did not fully love God. So they tithed and were still lovers of money? Following a rule of giving a percentage to God as an outward act does not mean that we are not still worshiping money in our hearts.

Historically, Christians through the years have always felt that 10% was what should go to the local church. Churches would be appropriately funded if we did this, as demonstrated by the financial abundance in the LDS church where its members are taught to tithe. Many of us who grew up in Christian homes were taught that we start there and increase as God allows. In the Old Testament, God did mandate a tithe to fund the tabernacle and temple ministry and pay the priests, but nowhere in the New Testament are non-Jews explicitly commanded to tithe. Frequently those who insist that New Testament Christians and those today are required to tithe reference Abraham's tithe in Genesis 14 which was before the law. I would encourage you to go and read that passage. It was a tenth of spoils of war, and it is the only reference to Abraham ever tithing.

I also want to point out that if you believe that the literal tithe is required for Christians today, I am certainly not going to try to talk you into giving less. In our home, we have never considered giving less than 10%. I do want to point something out to you though. If you believe that God requires 10%, and that is all you give anywhere, you are not actually generous. You are faithful, yes. And I commend you for that and God honors that. Good job. You are faithfully giving when very few today are. But don't confuse tithing, if you believe it is mandatory, with being generous. Generosity is never displayed by fulfilling requirements. Let me show you what I mean.

If you go out to dinner at a dine-in restaurant with a large party, they are likely going to add gratuity to your bill, right? When the server brings you the bill with the added gratuity displayed on it and you draw a line or write "$0" in the spot where you can write in additional gratuity, how crazy would it be for you to walk out thinking to yourself, "Wow, I am such a generous tipper! Look at what an enormous tip I left!" I think you'd be kidding yourself. That wasn't a generous tip. It was required. Mandated. You didn't have a choice. Generosity begins where the requirement ends.

So how much should you commit to give on your spending plan? A couple of thoughts I'd like to share as you search your heart and examine your income to make that determination. The amount you give should certainly show gratitude for how God has blessed you. If you tell your server at your favorite restaurant that you really appreciate his exemplary service and then leave him a lousy tip, what is the server going to think about your words of gratitude? The percentage we give to God should be a reflection of the gratitude in our hearts for what He has given to us.

The percentage we give should also show honor. God is the most deserving and precious One, and many times we treat him in such a dishonoring way in the way we approach giving ourselves or our resources to Him. When people ask me how much they should give in their situation, it is almost always about the minimum. What does that communicate? How do you think God *feels* when we ask that question? He does hear it, even if we just think it.

Look at it this way: If you are dating someone, or engaged or married, when your "significant other" had a birthday coming up, what if you went to them and asked: "What is the minimum amount of money I have to spend on you to show you that you are important to me? How cheap can I get out of this?" That is pretty *dis*-honoring, isn't it? Would you feel honored if someone approached you with that question?

If you asked someone you value to spend some time with you and they said, "I would love to. Tell me, though, what is the minimum that I need to spend with you to show you that you are important to me? I don't want to spend any more time with you than I have to." Ouch. But isn't that what many of us want to know when we talk about spending time with God? "How much time do I *have* to spend with God. What is the minimum?" Those who desire to be a part of

The Generosity Revolution would not be interested in finding out what the minimum required is. "I will do whatever it takes to be as generous as possible," not, "What is the least I can give (or more appropriately the most I can keep) and still be okay?"

I'll tell you how a simple budgeting practice has worked for many of people as a starting point. Think of all of your income in ten dollar increments. For every ten dollars you get, you could give one, save one, and live on the rest. Today most Christians, say, "God do you have change for a dollar? I want to give you a quarter." Seriously. 2.5% is the average. But more and more people are deciding to say, "God I can't keep $9 for me. I want to give you two or three dollars for every ten you give to me." We can show Him gratitude and honor by how we give.

Perhaps the single most important thing we should consider when seeking out what percentage to give is the statement we started with from Jesus. "Where your treasure is, there your heart will be also." If I believe that statement is true, then I need to give so much that my heart is pulled towards God and His kingdom, not to the world.

Once you decide how much you are going to give, you can then move on and fill out the rest of your spending plan. The plan we provided on our website has all of the categories you will likely need and some suggested percentages as a starting point. Once you get your income and expenses all listed out, you are ready to go. And, by the way, you are not our Federal

Government, so you need to have a balanced budget. The income and expenses need to match!

Two other encouragements for you: First, if you are married, both of you need to be involved in creating and adhering to the spending plan. Dave Ramsey, in his book *More Than Enough* has an excellent suggestion. The "nerd" who loves numbers should take the time to come up with the first draft, but the budget isn't final until it goes before and is approved by the "Budget Committee" which is the two of you. Work it out together. This will be challenging for some of you, but it is a good opportunity for you to practice healthy communication as you work through it. If both of you have the same goal of being as generous as possible, that will keep you motivated towards coming up with a suitable plan.

But I also want to encourage you to find someone outside of your household to be an accountability partner in your spending plan. Proverbs 11:14 reads, "Where there is no guidance the people fall, But in abundance of counselors there is victory." We need to lean on the wisdom of other people when it comes to deciding what is appropriate for us. There is always push-back from people when I share this. "Isn't what we give supposed to be a secret? Don't let your right hand know what your left hand is doing, right?" Go and read the passage where Jesus makes that statement in Matthew 6. Jesus clearly states that the point is to not do things to impress others, to try to earn their respect. That is not what I am talking about. I am talking about sharing your spending plan with someone you trust so that you can get another perspective on what you are doing. Don't use Jesus's words as an excuse to not have accountability when it comes to giving. Bring your finances into the light. Get a God-honoring plan in place.

Remember that it is not enough just to plan how you are going to use the money entrusted to you. You also need to track it to make sure that you are staying true to your commitment, whether this by writing it down or by using any of the electronic means available today like mint.com As I mentioned earlier, God is very good with His money and if we do not have any idea what happened to the money that He has already entrusted to us, I don't believe we should expect Him to put more of His resources under our care. Let's use the illustration of a financial advisor again. If you hired a financial firm to manage $10K, and when you got your statement and your balance was zero, how quickly would you call them? You'd be a little concerned. "What happened to my money?" you'd say, demanding an explanation. If their response was, "I have no idea what happened. I know what I did with some of it, but I have no idea what happened to the rest," would you give him more money to manage?

Do you know what you did with your last paycheck? Do you know what you did with the last raise that God gave you? If not, why would you expect Him to give you another one? Why would we expect Him to entrust us with more if we cannot give an account for what we have done with His previous investments with us? If you want to be a part of The Generosity Revolution, plan and track your spending. When you take the time to put together and follow a spending plan faithfully, you will cut down on waste and that will leave more money to use on others. If you decide to use future money wisely, why wouldn't God trust you with more? That's what He does!

There is so much we could do with the money that we may end up wasting. I want to share a story from Christmas a few years ago at the church where I serve. Just like where you live, we have many people struggling to provide gifts for their children at Christmas time. Over the last few years, we have provided gifts for mom's from a local transitional home that are trying to overcome their past choices. We also invite people who attend who are struggling to make ends meet to let us know so we can bless their kids

One couple picked a young single mom with a newborn off to bless and went over the top. They purchased her the following items from a local department store: an overstuffed chair, glider rocker, sofa table, lamps, wall and other decor, and a DVD player for the living room. They also bought a new wrought-iron bed, multiple sheet sets and beautiful comforter and accompanying toss pillows for her bedroom, and a comforter, bumpers, and four sets of sheets for the crib. They didn't stop there. They also gave her five cases of diapers in various sizes, clothes, and toys for the baby, $200 gift cards to Walmart and Target, a $200 gas card, paid all her utilities, and purchased new pajamas, robe, slippers, and gave her a gift certificate to a hair salon to have her hair done. Unbelievable? They still were not done. Add a vacuum, mop, broom, and microwave. They bought Pre-paid phone cards for 3 months, picture frames to match her decor, fixed the brakes on her car and purchased needed new front tires. They also gave her $400 cash to put into the bank for emergencies, and paid car insurance for 3 months! Can you imagine?

I don't think the young mom who received the gifts will forget Christmas of 2011. But do you know what? I don't think the givers will forget it either. As they look back over their life, I am sure they have spent that kind of money on themselves to purchase things that have broken or been replaced or upgraded. There was no lasting joy provided by those consumer purchases. But what they chose to do that Christmas will impact them forever too.

What if they hadn't planned and tracked their spending but just spent everything that came in as so many people do? They would have missed out on the experience of changing this young family's life. For those of you who are blessed with significant income, have you ever done anything like that? Maybe we could all add a line item to our budget that would be an "others" category where we can set aside some money every month just to bless people.

Some of you may not ever have enough extra to do something this extravagant. Not everyone has the type of income that would allow us to save up to do

something like that, but certainly you could bless someone with some of your extra. That will only happen if
we plan and track our spending so our extra doesn't
disappear by spending it just on ourselves.

HEART CHECK

I hope by now that you truly desire to be generous, to truly place God first in your spending plan. After putting the amount that you want to give first, when you list everything else that you have to and want to spend in all of the other categories, there is a really good chance that you are going to end up with a negative number at the end after the first draft. You will likely have to go back and make some cuts. The question is, what do you cut?

Andy Stanley wrote a great book entitled *When Work and Family Collide*. It is a great book that talks about the work/life balance. If you are someone who has a family and you work, you probably struggle between the two. His point in the book is: we are going to cheat somewhere. We aren't going to always have the time to do everything we want to do, so we have to make a conscious choice that one of them will occasionally be sacrificed on the altar of the other. He suggests, instead of choosing to cheat our family as so many do, we should choose to cheat our work. He says that our family can tell when they are not the priority. No matter what we say, they can sense if they are not first.

As you think about your finances, do you think God can tell if He isn't the most important? You are never going to have enough money to do everything. If we are going to choose to cheat, and we have to, why not cheat our kingdom instead of God's? If you need to make a revision to your first (and maybe second and third!) draft of your spending plan, I would encourage you to try to cut from all of the other categories where you can first and then only reduce your giving if all other cuts have been made. You may have to pull back your giving for a time and that is okay. As you stay faithful, you will be able to raise it again in the future. What is your ultimate priority? Building God's kingdom or your own. You really cannot serve two masters. Your spending plan will either reflect that God is clearly the most important or it will display that He is not. Let's put Him first in everything.

Chapter Four

STEP 3

AVOID CONSUMER DEBT

In Matthew 25, Jesus tells a parable known as the parable of the talents. In it, Jesus illustrates that we are simply managers of what belongs to God and that He expects us to bear fruit with it — to invest it in ways that will benefit the owner's wealth.

He shares that the kingdom of heaven is like a landowner who went away on journey and entrusts to each person an amount to manage according to his own ability. The picture He is illustrating is that God entrusts a different amount to each one of us, dependent on our ability to manage it and ultimately to determine if we are able to handle more.

In the parable, when the owner returned and called the three managers to give an account for what they had done with the money entrusted to them, the first two demonstrate that they invested wisely and grew their master's resources. They were called good and faithful stewards and were entrusted with more responsibility. They had proven themselves worthy of trust.

The third steward was not so faithful. In fact, he was

called wicked and lazy because he simply returned what was the master's money to him without investing it wisely and causing it to grow. He did not lose what was the master's; he simply did not invest it wisely which was clearly the expectation.

I want you to think on something for a moment. Whom are you most like? What if today you stood before the Owner to give an account for how you have used the resources He has entrusted to you? What would His response be?

The sad thing is that many of us have created an unthinkable fourth scenario in which we have placed ourselves. If the master returned today and asked us to give an account, many of us would have nothing to return to Him at all. We have spent all that was His on ourselves!

But in reality that is not all some of us have done. We have taken it a step further. Instead of multiplying God's money as He intended, we have not only spent what He entrusted to us, but we have actually placed Him in debt. Imagine what the owner would have said to the servant if he would have returned and called him to give and account and, rather than returning the money with interest or even the original amount by itself, the servant handed him a stack of credit card bills and a car (or I guess chariot) payment! Such a scenario would seem absurd to Jesus's audience, but it has become completely normal for our day. If God is the owner of the money we possess as we saw in Chapter Two, then by going into debt with His money, we have placed the

God of the universe in debt to our creditors! If Jesus was so harsh with this man who simply returned what had been entrusted to Him without increasing it, what would God say to those of us who have lost it all and put our Master in bondage?

If we want to be a part of The Generosity Revolution, we've got to avoid consumer debt. If you are in debt, you will not be able to be as generous as you want to be. That is a fact. When you are in debt, you are no longer free to do as you please or as you feel God is leading you. Proverbs 22:7 says, "The rich rules over the poor, and the borrower becomes the lender's slave."

Is that really true? Are you a slave to those to whom you owe? Absolutely. You have subjected yourself to them. We are supposed to be slaves of Jesus Christ, not Visa™, American Express™ and Toyota Motor Credit Corporation™. How can you sincerely come to God and ask Him what He wants you to do with His money if you've pre-obligated so much of it to other institutions?

Debt takes away our options. If you are strapped financially with debt, you are trapped. You are enslaved. You can't do the things that you feel like God is calling you to do with money because you've already strapped yourself to payments.

Some of you might say that you are okay being a slave because you enjoy the stuff that your debt has given you. Being a slave feels pretty good for a time if it gets you what you want, doesn't it? But for those of us who are followers of Jesus, we have to look at the Bible and ask ourselves if going into debt for stuff we don't really need is what God wants for us. Is He okay with it? Does the Bible give us any indication for how God would view our widespread willingness to subject ourselves to financial bondage?

Perhaps the clearest verse in the New Testament on the issue of consumer debt is Romans 13:8. The Apostle Paul writes, "Owe nothing to anyone except to love one another; for he who loves his neighbor has fulfilled the law." Let me ask you something that may catch you off guard: Do you view that verse as a suggestion or a command? I am not sure why this is, but I think sometimes we treat the statements on handling money in the Bible as tips — take it or leave it — as if God is just giving us some advice on a radio show, but not actually giving an instruction.

I can't figure out why we view this as a suggestion. Paul begins Romans 13 with instruction on submitting to authority. I've never talked to anyone or read any commentary that shared the view that the instruction to submit to the governing authorities is a suggestion. No way. That would be ridiculous. Then Paul starts talking about money in relationship to authority when he addresses paying taxes to those authorities. Again, I've never heard anyone say that Paul is making a suggestion here. And then we come to "Owe nothing to anyone except to love one another." Is that a command or a suggestion?

I admit it is difficult to think this through when you consider a home mortgage, debt to expand a business, or school loans. In our culture today, debt for those things seems almost unavoidable and in many cases it is. In a housing situation, you are going to owe someone, whether it is being legally bound in a lease or in a mortgage, so it is just a matter of which is more wise. In these instances, I believe we should exercise extreme caution when we have to borrow, borrow as little as possible and then pay it back as quickly as possible. We really must be cautious to not use these problem areas as a smokescreen to justify borrowing for things that we do not need.

Let's avoid consumer debt. We are robbing ourselves of the opportunity to give and robbing the would-have-been recipients of our generosity. Make a decision today not to borrow for consumer purchases any more. It really is a decision we can make, but in order to change our ways, we need to talk through the reasons why we go into debt. Obviously there are times that there are unplanned emergencies that can drive us into debt. Even if you are well-prepared, you cannot be prepared for every possible event. Medical emergencies can quickly eat up our savings. But let's focus on consumer debt which is the biggest problem affecting most of us. "Why do people go into consumer debt?" This is an obvious answer, but you'll see my point. People go into debt because there is something that they want (or believe that they need) that they don't have. Jesus taught us how to pray and said that we are to rely on God for our daily bread, our physical needs (Matthew 6:11). On what are we relying to meet our needs, and our wants, now?

One of the pastors on our staff traveled to India a few years ago to visit some Mercy Homes (www.mercy-homes.org) that we support. The people he met there have so little. He was amazed at how badly they wanted to be prayed for. That's what they wanted. They would line up for hours just so Gary could pray for their needs.

If they had any kind of sickness, they wanted prayer, even for the little curable things, like a headache. Why don't we seek prayer like that? We've got Tylenol. They can't afford Tylenol, so they turn to God. Why don't we pray for our daily bread anymore? Because if things get tight, we can just charge it. When we desire something, we used to come to God and pray that He would provide it. Now we just borrow to get it. We need to get back to putting our confidence in God instead of in our credit score or our credit line. Right now, when He doesn't give us what we want, we can find another way.

If God hasn't given you the cash to purchase something, then maybe we should not buy it. God has the power to provide what we need by providing the resources for us to have it. I don't believe that credit lines and credit cards are God's way of providing for us. They are our way of going around God's provision for us. Can you think of a passage anywhere in the Bible where God "provided" for someone by extending them a credit line? I can't think of a single occurrence. One of the great stories of God's provision is in the Old Testament book of 2 Kings. There was a widow in 2 Kings 4 that owed people money and didn't have the means to pay, a perfect story to reference in a chapter about the pitfalls of being in debt. She came to Elisha the prophet for help. Go and read the story for yourself if you are unfamiliar with it. He didn't give her a loan. That wouldn't be helping her. Loaning money to people doesn't help them. He gave her income. If God wants you to have something, He will give you the money. We can never be as generous as possible if we continue to live with consumer debt.

Think of how generous we could be if we didn't owe money. How much more generous you could personally be if you did not have debt? We need to avoid consumer debt if we are going to be as generous as we can be with the money God has entrusted to us. In the Good Sense Budget Course, one of their key questions is "How much of God's money do I need to live on?" The idea is to figure out how much we need to consume and then simply give away the rest. The amount we will need to keep to live on will be way less if we stop paying interest.

I would encourage you to sit down and figure out how much your consumer debt is actually costing you. Most American families are throwing away hundreds of dollars a month, just because they couldn't wait until God provided the money for them to buy things that they didn't really need to begin with. Maybe put this book down and go get your credit statements and add up the total of your payments right now. How different would your financial situation be if you didn't have so much going to debt payments every month? What could you do with that extra money if you had waited until you had the money and paid cash?

I want to address a particular area that can release tens of thousands of dollars from your budget would enable to you be far more generous than you could imagine. Some of you may think that in our day, you are just going to have to borrow for houses and for cars. Those two just get frequently lumped together, but they are two completely separate categories. Over time, borrowing for a house is frequently, although not always, a wise move. Cars should not be treated as a similar category. Yes, most of us need our own transportation, but we can avoid car payments. Yes, you heard it right. It is possible to live in our current times without a car payment. I would guess that most of us have spent way more than we needed to in order to enjoy driving a brand-new car. We have done that in our household in the past too, and I regret it deeply.

Cars are a major expense in our lifetime. What if you could pay cash for your cars? Some of you think, "How in the world could I do that?" If you have a payment, finish paying it off and then drive the car until you have enough cash to buy your next car. "Who does that?" you might ask. People who want to be as generous as possible do. Even if you just took out a car loan, spend the first five years paying off the car you bought and the next five saving for the next car. And then you won't have to make payments to anyone for a car again!

It is incredibly unwise to borrow money for a never-owned vehicle. Cars depreciate in value so fast that they are never wise to borrow for them. If you got a tip about this hot new stock that was guaranteed to drop by 10% to 20% the next day, would you rush to invest? Of course not. If you knew the housing market was going to go down, would you rush to get into a house with payments you could barely afford? Obviously the answer is no, but that is exactly what you are doing when you buy a brand-new, never-owned car. You are taking some of God's money and putting into an investment that loses 10% - 20% the moment you drive it off the lot. And unlike good stocks or mutual funds, there is no chance of you ever recovering that money. The stock market fluctuates in value, but the value of automobiles is a sharp decline right away, with a steady decline from then on.

This is one of the reasons why even a 0% loan on a new car is unwise. You are still taking a 15 - 20% hit right away. You are spending 15 - 20% to get a 0% loan. In addition, you do not know for sure that you will be able to make every payment on time, do you? And if you default at all, your interest rate skyrockets. This is the same reason why should avoid no interest loans or "no payments, no interest for-a-time" loans for furniture, electronics, appliances and other items. People think, "If I am not paying interest it is okay to be in debt." But you still have the payments. Are you absolutely sure of the future and that you will be able to make the payments? Do you think all of those lenders are looking out for the consumer's best interest when they offer such loans? I assure you they are not. They are looking to make money. A majority of people are unable to pay off their "interest free" loans and end up suffering under enormous interest fees. You could be one of those people. Avoid consumer debt. Any consumer debt.

Just to clarify, yes, borrowing for a used car is not as bad of financial hit as doing so for a new one, but we still pay about 15 - 20% more than the sticker price when you finance a used car and pay it off over the suggested time. Why would any of us think that paying 15 - 20% more than it is worth for anything is a good move? When you go grocery shopping, do you ask them to add 20% to your bill? "I like to pay 20% more for things. That's the way I roll." And we wonder why God doesn't trust us with more. The average car payment in America is $464. If you invested that money into retirement and earned a 10% return on average, you would retire with over $3 million dollars! You could live on some and be incredibly generous with the rest! If you have a car payment right now, finish paying it off and then drive the car until you save enough cash to buy your next car.

Let's avoid consumer debt in the future. What do we do with the consumer debt we have right now? Get aggressive in paying it off. Dave Ramsey suggests that you get $1000 in the bank for emergencies and then go crazy to get out of debt.

Maybe you need to go back over your spending plan and put more on debt. Perhaps this year you shouldn't go on such an extravagant vacation. That is money you could use to payoff your debts. You should probably concede the neighborhood Christmas-decorating contest to someone else this year because you are going to put the money you would have spent on the decorations and increased electricity bills toward debt.

You figure out how much you can put on your credit cards and other loans and you get those paid off. Ramsey calls it the debt snowball. You pay as much as possible on your lowest balance debt and your minimum payments on everything else. Once the smallest debt is paid, you add what you were paying on the smallest debt to the next smallest debt. Once that is paid you add that to your next debt until you are free.

Even if you don't desire to give more but just want to get rich, being in debt is foolish. Dave Ramsey points out that The Forbes 400, who are the 400 wealthiest people say becoming and staying debt free is the number one key to building wealth.

If we want to be free to give more tomorrow, we've got to stop borrowing money for things we don't need today. Don't do it. No matter what. Make a decision not to borrow. Debt is killing our options. It is robbing us of the freedom that Jesus purchased for us. You never know what opportunity you will have with the freedom you experience when you get your debts paid off. I received this email from a young lady who is part of our church family.

I just wanted to thank you for your heart for the Pursuiters and discipleship. I will be honest, I do not believe I would be where I am in life if it weren't for God using you and you being open to God's voice. Especially in the financial area. It wasn't your first or even 2nd sermon on finances that got me, it was the continuous growth in all of them. I remember each time being convicted in little ways and getting better and better. One in particular, however, really got me. I had a good paying job with Farmers at the time, was living in a really nice apartment on my own. I could afford my lifestyle and was working to get out of debt, but I was convicted to work harder and give up my nice lifestyle to live much simpler to get out of debt faster. Not long after that, God called me into missions.

In one year, I paid off over $15,000 in debt and am almost completely debt free. I do not think I would have been released into missions had that not happened. Well, honestly, I wouldn't have been able to afford to be a missionary had I not gotten it all paid off. It has saved me thousands in interest. It also prepared me for a much simpler life style than what I dreamed of, which is good because I'm going to have to live simply from here on out. I'm okay with that because I realized in that time I really didn't miss all the things our society tells us we need.

I know sometimes it must get frustrating and you must feel like a broken record, but it really helped me. Even after all of that, I still struggle with materialism but at least I know how to battle it better. So THANKS!

Today she is on the mission field, making every second of her life count for eternity. She is living The Generosity Revolution! She could not be doing what she is doing today if she was still strapped by debt. What should we do? Commit to owe no one anything except love. You decide today, right now, that you are going to submit your finances to God and do what He says.

Heart Check

Which should we do first, give or pay down debt?
That depends. Do we want God's help in paying off
our debt? Then we give to Him what He deserves first,
and then pay off debt. Remember the passage from
Malachi 3 we discussed in Chapter 1, where God tells
them they are cursed because they are not giving? What
does He tell them to do?

*"Bring the whole tithe into the storehouse, so that there
may be food in My house, and test Me now in this," says
the LORD of hosts, "if I will not open for you the windows
of heaven and pour out for you a blessing until it overflows"*
(Malachi 3:10).

God tells the people of Israel that since they aren't
giving Him what they are supposed to, He is making
their financial life a wreck. He loves us too much to
allow us to put Him second and trust in our own abilities rather than His ability to provide. Don't try to get
out of debt without God's help. Give first to Him so
you invite Him to help.

It is not your church's fault that you are in debt. It
isn't the fault of the family in need that God has put in
your path to bless. It is not God's fault you are in debt.
Don't rob God and your eternal inheritance by taking
it out of giving. Don't rob your earthly future by taking
it from retirement savings. Let's take our increased debt

payments out of our spending money. Be aggressive in getting out of debt, but also remain committed to giving the full percentage you are supposed to give to God while doing so. Be generous now while getting out of debt so that God can bless us so we can get out of debt quicker in order to be even more generous in the future.

GENEROSITY REVOLUTION

Chapter Five

STEP 4

SAVE INTENTIONALLY

It was several years ago that I first participated in Willow Creek's "Good Sense Budget Course." I laughed when they clarified that saving 50% on a sweater at a department store is not saving, but it is actually spending. "Do people really think that way?" I thought to myself. Actually, I think they do.

Do you notice how many cash register receipts at department stores and even grocery stores highlight how much you "saved?" Sometimes that information is more prominent than the total spent. At one national department store where we shop regularly that is known for their great sales, whenever we are handed the receipt, the cashier has been trained to say, "Congratulations! You just saved 'x' amount of dollars." I've never said it since there is no way it would not come off as rude, but I feel like saying, "I didn't save anything. I spent money. I save money when I put it in the bank." For many of us in our culture, savings off of the original price is the only type of saving we ever do. To be a part of The Generosity Revolution, we need to save intentionally.

Some of you might say, "I can't afford to save money. You don't know my situation." The truth is, we can't afford not to save, no matter what our current financial situation is. If we are receiving any income, we need get into the habit of saving every time we do. Proverbs 21:10 says, "In the house of the wise are stores of choice food and oil, but a foolish man devours all he has." There it is straight from the Bible. It doesn't say rich people save. It says wise people save. People who consume everything that comes in are financially foolish. There are wise people who make little money and there are wise people who make a lot. It isn't how much money we make that shows if we are wise, but rather what we do with the money that comes in.

What does saving money have to do with generosity? The most obvious reason is that when opportunities arrive to give toward a big project, whether that be local or a missions opportunity, we can't give big if we haven't saved big. I received this email from someone who was able to give big to our church a couple of years ago.

"For several years now our two girls and I have tagged along with my husband to Phoenix, Arizona on his work trips, so it has become one of our favorite places to visit. We have been talking extensively for about a year and a half about buying a condo in the area, believing that we will not only we be able to enjoy it, but that it will be a great long-term investment.

We started to look at properties a few months ago and made full price offers on three different properties and each time, there were numerous offers on each condo so our offer was not accepted. We were disappointed, but we were certain that the Lord had other plans even though we weren't sure what they were.

That next Sunday, when you mentioned giving appreciated stock to campus development to expand our impact in the valley, our 17-year-old daughter leaned over and said, "We should give the condo money to the church." She voiced precisely what was running through my mind, but my husband was at home with kidney stones so now I just needed to go home and let him know that I felt God was leading us to donate that money to the church.

I wanted to share the message with him as best I could, and then see if he was having the same thoughts as I was, but our daughter was so excited that she just blurted it out before I could say anything. After explaining the message, thankfully, he was on board! We both felt convicted that things of this earth were not to be our treasure, and that if we gave our condo money to the church then it would contribute more greatly to building God's Eternal Kingdom. Not only were both of us on board and very excited, but our girls were too.

They had set aside money for a specific purpose, but God had something else in mind. If debt limits our options, as we stated in the last chapter, having money in savings expands them. When there is money in the bank that we have diligently saved, we have more opportunities to be generous when great causes present themselves.

Have you ever been made aware of a cause that was so compelling that it just overwhelmed you? Do you remember having the thought, "I wish I had more money to help, because I'd give it." There are millions trapped as sexual slaves, many of whom are children. Around 28,000 kids die from preventable deaths every day around the world. There are villages full of people whose only drinking water is so filthy that I would not let my kids even step in it with their bare feet.

What is it that burdens you? Is it that there are orphans waiting to be adopted and parents waiting to adopt that don't have the resources to do so? Is it the single mom you know who is struggling to provide gifts for her children? If you are a follower of Jesus, something has to burden you. Are you in a position financially to help do something about it? You can be someday if you start saving intentionally.

Even if God never calls you to make a significant donation with money you have saved, it is still an important piece of The Generosity Revolution. Why? We can avoid future debt. If you don't have the money in the bank to cover "surprise" expenses, how else will you pay for them? I put "surprise" in quotes for a reason. Most of the unexpected expenses that "surprise" us would not have been surprises if we would have stopped and thought through our life situation ahead of time.

You have probably heard that you should save for emergencies, but most emergencies don't have to be emergencies. We need to save for emergencies and for long term goals like retirement and the college fund, but we can avoid emergencies by also saving for replacing the things we know are going to break.

As you look to the future, what are some expenses that you are going to face in the next five to ten years? You need to take inventory of all that is under your care and build a spreadsheet or form a list of what is likely to break or need replacing and start saving now to pay for them when the time comes. You do know that everything you own is going to break or need to be replaced eventually, right? How are you going to pay for these things if you don't establish the discipline of saving up for them now?

Our cultural habit is to just borrow to pay for these expenses for which we could have been prepared by saving up money in advance. As we mentioned in the last chapter, we should be saving up money to replace our current vehicles. How else are we going to pay for them? Our only option if we don't save up the money ahead of time is more years of debt payments afterwards. What about braces for your kids, the birth or adoption of a child, or a new roof for your home? What appliances are starting to show their age? We must save up for these things or we will be put back into slavery, causing us to throw away more of God's money in interest, and robbing us of the opportunity to give. In our household, we use one savings account but we use a spreadsheet to keep track of the different amounts in each area of savings. We regularly set aside money for car replacement, medical deductibles, appliance replacement, and vacations. Are you currently saving for these things? If we save up money for them, then as I mentioned in Chapter 2, we can actually rejoice when expenses come up and we have the money in the bank. We don't have to be excited that we have the expenses, but rather that God provided the income we needed and the wisdom to set some of the money aside. Emergencies don't have to be catastrophic if the money is in the bank.

Replacement savings is so important if we want to live on as little of God's money as possible. Sit down and figure out how much money, not just in payments, but just what you spend in interest every month. You may want to do that in the bathroom in case you have to vomit! Do you realize that collectively we spend more in interest on consumer purchases than we give to God's work in the world? I would encourage you to look and see if that is true in your household. If we would have established the discipline of saving money every month and simply waited until we had the money and paid cash for the things for which we currently borrowed to attain, we could have been giving to God, changing lives and investing in heaven, at the same out of pocket cost to us!

Many of us could currently be giving hundreds of dollars more every month but we instead are throwing it away on interest because we couldn't wait until we had the money to upgrade our lifestyle. The only way to avoid interest when you make purchases in the future is to start saving intentionally now so that you can save up enough money ahead of time to pay cash. We need to establish a habit of saving every time we receive income. If you don't have that habit established, set it up as an automatic transfer so you don't have a chance to spend it first.

I want you to think differently about saving. Saving is future spending. Having a big savings account gives you options! Income is opportunity; if you blow it all, you will miss out on opportunity. Financially foolish people spend, spend, spend until there is a crash and then they stop because they have to. Financially wise people save, save, save during seasons of plenty so that when there is a crash, they have the opportunity to purchase at the reduced prices. How many of you had the thought, "If only I had $10K in the bank that I could invest in the stock market right now" when a company's stock or the market as a whole dropped? The only way you are going to be able to take advantage of the deals at the next crash is if you save intentionally.

How many people stretched themselves so thin to get in a no money down or interest only or adjustable rate mortgage? Now they are paying for it dearly. What if they would have done the wise, but unpopular thing, of save, save, save for a down payment? If you would have done that in the last several years instead of buying your house a couple of years ago, you could take your pick on a great house at a great price right now.

Wise people save, but it is also wise to be cautious how we invest. Ecclesiastes 5:13-14 says, "There is a grievous evil which I have seen under the sun: riches being hoarded by their owner to his hurt. When those riches were lost through a bad investment and he had fathered a son, then there was nothing to support him." If it sounds too good to be true, it probably is. Don't fall for the many get-rich-quick schemes that are out there. Wise people also diversify their savings. Ecclesiastes 11:2 tell us, "Divide your portion to seven, or even to eight, for you do not know what misfortune may occur on the earth." There is no one sure thing. Spread out your savings.

There are several categories for which we should save. In addition to replacement savings, a wise first step is to get savings in the bank for emergencies. As I mentioned in the last chapter, as a starting point for your emergency savings, Dave Ramsey in his Total Money Makeover recommends that the first thing you want to get in the bank is $1000 for emergency savings. Do this right away. Sell some stuff if you have to. Put yourself on a spending freeze. Cancel your next weekend trip. Do whatever you need to do to get $1000 in the bank immediately. That will allow you to handle the things that are going to go wrong with your car or your house in the next few months. Then you can start getting aggressive in paying off debt.

Once your consumer debt is paid off, then you can begin to aggressively save. Wise financial planners suggests that you should have three to six months of your expenses (not your income) in the bank for emergencies. This is a flexible guideline. You should look at your income and life situation and determine what is right for you. What are the possibilities of layoffs in your industry? There are some industries where layoffs are so common that six months may not be enough. In your position, you may see losing your income as extremely unlikely through a layoff but that does not mean you should not have money in the bank. What if you had an injury or some physical condition that prevented you from working for a time? Don't dismiss this by thinking it couldn't happen to you. Many others have thought they were immune and therefore failed to prepare. Husbands and fathers, or single moms, you owe it to your family to make sure that if something happened to your job, you could still take care of your family while you are finding a new job. 1 Timothy 5:8 warns us, "But if anyone does not provide for his own, and especially for those of his household, he has denied the faith and is worse than an unbeliever." We normally think of this just in reference to earning money, but this would certainly apply to planning for emergencies and future needs by saving.

There are times when unexpected events occur that can put us in a financial bind, and we are forced to depend on those outside of ourselves. I believe that one of the reasons that God allows these times in our lives is to teach us humility and to prevent us from believing that we do not need other people.

However, if I am a part of The Generosity Revolution, then I need to put myself in a position where I do not need to lean on others when it is unnecessary. It is our responsibility to provide for ourselves and those who rely on us. If circumstances outside of my control put us in need, then that allows the generosity of others to be appropriately used on me. That's what family and the church is for, to come around each other during our times of struggle.

But if I fail to work hard and earn the income or had the income to meet my own needs and failed to plan and save appropriately, then when I am in need and depend on others' generosity, I am actually robbing those who were truly in need. Money that could have gone to feed those who live in poverty around the world instead is given to me because I overspent or didn't save appropriately. We must save intentionally.

The biggest priority for which we should all be saving is any long-term goals like retirement or college savings for your children. There are significant tax advantages to doing this, but the biggest advantage is the money you make with compound interest. It is not just the money you put in that earns interest; the interest you earn starts earning interest, which earns interest, which earns interest, etc. Go online and find a savings and investment calculator and figure out how much your money can grow if you save over time. Time is your best friend when it comes to saving. Start as soon as possible. Let me give you an example. If you wait until you are 35 to start saving for retirement and you save $100 a month and earn an average of 10% per year, at 65 you would have $207,929. Not bad for only $36,000 invested. But, if you start saving when you are 25 and save $100 a month and average a 10% return and then stop saving when you are 35 and just leave that money alone, you will have $209,393! Would you rather save $100 for ten years or for thirty years to yield the same return? As you can see, it really is not in your best interest to spend all that we get. If we are not saving money, we are throwing away much more of it. If we add together the two previous examples, if you start at 25 and contribute $100 per month and average a 10% return until age 65, it yields $559,461. Your contribution would be just $48,000. That is the beauty of compound interest.

This is why the second best thing you can do with money, and the second priority on our spending plan is to set some of it aside and keep putting it in the bank. Everything around us screams at us to consume. Walking through the mall and seeing the latest outfit in the window, the commercials on TV, the car that zips by you, everything seems to want us to give into the temptation and spend. I really believe that Satan is trying to distract us so we miss out on what we could do for God's kingdom if we saved money intentionally.

We've got to see through the tricks of consumerism. Imagine if you were in a weight loss competition with your friend, competing for a prize. If your friend really wants the prize, they are likely going to put candy bars on your desk, order you a late night pizza as a gift, and offer you a few of their fries if you go out to eat together. You would snicker and smile every time he or she offered. You'd say, "No way. I know what you are trying to do." Honestly, that is how we should respond to the tricks to try to get us to spend. Don't fall for it.

Call out the tricks as traps and remind yourself that you are called to be an investor, not a consumer. Save intentionally. I need to warn you that once you have money in the bank for a specific purpose, it can be very tempting to use that money for lesser purposes if they present themselves. When I first started teaching the Good Sense Budget Course, I always encouraged people who were taking the class because they wanted to get out of debt to make sure they come and take the class again once they were out of debt and started having a surplus. The only thing harder than being a good money manager when you don't have any extra money is being a good money manager when you do! When you have the money sitting there, suddenly there are many more things you can afford, and there will be a temptation to move those savings categories into spending money. Don't do it. Stay intentional as you save.

I do want to say one more thing on saving. If you make that your first goal instead of your second, you are not being obedient and will not be as generous as you could be. Money can easily tether us if it remains in our possession and too much of it is going to our future kingdom through saving. Before we stockpile money, we ought to remind ourself that money can tether our hearts. Take some time and read Luke 12:13-21. Jesus tells a parable of a man who thought saving money for the future was the top priority, and He was called a fool. We are to save for our needs, but we are not to hoard beyond what we need. Those who are a part of

The Generosity Revolution understand that if we save up too much, we will not be able to be as generous as possible.

Heart Check

Saving up for specific things is a great blessing. Once you establish the discipline, it can actually become quite addicting. In fact, I would argue from experience that saving money and seeing those totals move up, bringing you closer to your goal, is as much fun as spending, maybe even more so. But I have to warn you: there may come a time when God asks you to surrender the money that you have so diligently stock-piled for that purchase for a greater purpose. What do you do when God asks you to give what you had designated for saving towards future spending?

We consider ourselves to be generous. I feel like we sacrifice in making less of a salary than is rightfully mine and in what we choose to give. Several years ago we put some money in a stock, and it grew by several thousand dollars. We felt like God was giving back to us, that this was one of the ways He was going to provide for us to show His faithfulness for all of the generosity in our past.

After a few years of watching it grow, I believed that God was telling me to put more in because He was going to double it. I want to be clear that this was not normal for me and I would not suggest using that as an excuse if you are trying to convince a spouse or a friend of an investment opportunity, but I genuinely felt peace about it. I was now convinced that He was really going to bless us for how generous we have been.

It totally made sense. That's the way God is.

We always planned on being generous and giving our normal percentage generous percentage when we sold it but then we had our own plans of what to do with the part that we kept. At the beginning of 2011, I was preaching a sermon where I challenged our church family to lay everything on the table so-to-speak and pray, "God anything you want, you can have it." Literally, as I was urging Pursuiters to do that, I laid my hands out in front of me symbolizing that I was saying it to God along with them.

As I said that, God said to me. "I want the stock. I want it all. I know you had plans for it, but I am going to use all of that to help reach people here." It wasn't a great time for me to have a debate with God since I was in the middle of my sermon, so I picked up the conversation with Him after I was done preaching that service. I wish I could tell you that I responded with excitement, with eagerness to give that money. But my first response was, "Seriously? We're already generous. You know what already we give. You know what we keep. We were going to use that for our next car."

God just asked me if I trusted Him. He asked me what really was most important to me. After hesitating for a little bit, I surrendered it all. Even though I surrendered everything within a few minutes of processing it completely, it really bothered me that I hesitated as I preached the remaining three services that day. When God called me to give more than I had planned, my response was not as enthusiastic as I had hoped or expected.

It hit me that afternoon. "If I hesitate, with what I've committed to The Pursuit as its lead and founding pastor, what must it be like for everyone else?" I know that there will probably be some hesitation in all of us at times to give as God is calling us to. Even though we can declare that we want to be as generous as possible, there are times when our enthusiasm wanes as we consider other options for that money. Don't beat yourself up over hesitating. Don't feel bad if you are hoping that there is some other way.

Do you remember what Jesus prayed in the garden of Gethsemane? Right before He was crucified, knowing the price God was calling Him to pay, he said this: "My Father, if it is possible, let this cup pass from Me; yet not as I will, but as You will" (Matthew 26:39).

If Jesus was hoping there was some other way, it is okay for us to want that too sometimes. We should also follow Jesus's example though. When the Father reminded Him that the cross was the only way, He took up His cross and was crucified. So give yourself grace that maybe being as generous as possible isn't always going to be easy, but then take the step of faith knowing God is faithful.

Chapter Six

STEP 5

USE CASH WHENEVER POSSIBLE

I'm sure some of you may be thinking you could probably skip this chapter. You may be wondering why it
is even in here. What does this have to do with being
generous? Please don't skip this step. This is a key
opportunity for you who desire to be a part of The
Generosity Revolution to free up additional funds to
give away without even really noticing. There are actually multiple reasons why using cash whenever possible
is so important.

The first and probably the most obvious reason for
using cash is that there is no risk of going into debt
when you do. It puts a definite limit to your spending. If you use cash and you don't have any more cash
available, you don't have anything to spend. Brilliant,
huh? But honestly, this is small potatoes compared to
the other benefits.

The second reason why I am encouraging you to use
cash whenever possible is because of the ease of tracking
your spending in categories. As I mentioned in Chapter
Three, having a plan for how you are going to spend

your money is great, but without a way to track your spending, your plan is nothing more than a plan and will not necessarily reflect reality.

Using cash is the easiest way to track your spending to make sure you are staying on course with your plan. When you receive your income, you check your spending plan and withdraw the money you have pre-decided and put the appropriate amount into each of your labeled envelopes. You can buy nice envelopes and even keep them in an organizer if you'd like, but simple mailing envelopes in a drawer can work just fine too.

You will want to have an envelope for Entertainment, Clothing, Snacks, Allowance, Groceries, Household, etc. It is important to have an envelope for whatever categories there are on your spending plan where using cash is possible. You do not need to have an envelope for your rent, mortgage, or utilities because you likely pay those directly from your checking account or online. Many people find it beneficial to combine Groceries and Household if you regularly shop at stores where you buy groceries and household items together so you do not need to take two envelopes and break your purchase into two separate orders when you visit these stores.

I have to pause right now to clarify something before you are tempted (again!) to jump to the next chapter. This is not just for beginners, the mathematically challenged, or those who can't use a spreadsheet. Likewise, it is not just a temporary tool you use until you get a handle on your finances. I suggest that you make this a life-long habit that you start developing today. Dave Ramsey is a multi-millionaire and he uses cash in envelopes for his day-to-day expenses. (I imagine his envelopes are a lot thicker than yours and mine, but you've got to respect the discipline!) This can work for everyone.

Let's use your entertainment budget as an example. At the beginning of the month, you would put the amount of cash decided for that category on your spending plan in an envelope, whether it is $40, $200 or $500. This practice works no matter how much you choose to spend. Every time you decide to go out to eat or catch a movie, you would simply grab the cash from that envelope to use and then return any change to that envelope at the end of the day. You are free to spend whatever you want in that category until the envelope runs out. The envelope provides freedom with safe limits.

I want to warn you. At the beginning of your first month, it is feels like you struck gold when you go to that fat envelope and imagine all of the places you could go and things you could do with all of that money. But after a couple of nights on the town, that envelope doesn't feel so thick any more. Now when you go to the envelope, you are searching frantically through all of the bills hoping there is a $20 bill somewhere amongst all of the fives, ones and loose change from the previous events. You will probably blow through your money pretty fast at the beginning, but somewhere in the month, you are going to think about going out to eat and you are going to go pick up the envelope.

When you open it up and see there is not much in there and you still have several days left in the month, you'll think twice before you go out, and suddenly leftovers from last night starts to sound like a pretty good option for dinner. There is no better and simpler way to track your expenses and stay within the boundaries you set for yourself in your spending plan than by using cash.

But as a part of The Generosity Revolution, these are not the biggest reasons to use cash. Here's a fact for you of which you've probably never thought. We will have more money with which we can be generous if we use cash. How can I say that? We end up spending less over the long run when we use cash for daily purchases whenever possible.

Study after study has been done on this. If you use a debit or credit card when you go to the grocery store or mall, you are likely spending 12 - 18% more than you would if you were using cash. Spending 12 - 18% more on purchases to get 1 or 2% cash back is not a good financial strategy. You can be really bad at math and still recognize that.

Here's the problem with using plastic. Using a credit or debit card when you make a purchase is like getting an epidural when you are having a baby. Something is passing out of you, but you don't feel it leaving! We need to feel the pain when we spend. Signing our name and walking away gives us no sense that we have lost anything, but handing over some bills and getting a little change back does.

I have had people protest using cash because they

believe that they would spend it too fast. "When I have cash, it burns a hole in my pocket," they say. That may be true, but only for the first month. After you have burned through your fun money on the 7th and have the rest of the month to sit at home while your friends are watching that new release movie that everyone wants to see, you will figure it out. You will soon start to bypass purchases early in the month because you'll learn from your mistakes. Over time, when the cash pile for the month starts getting lower, you will start slowing down your spending.

Would you try it? I fought this idea when I first heard it. I loved collecting frequent flier miles, and I really was convinced that it would not make a difference with me. I had convinced myself that I was disciplined enough to think through the consequences when I spent with a credit card, but I was consistently having a little too much month left over at the end of my money, as Dave Ramsey says, so I decided to try it. Do you know what happened? Instantly I had money left over at the end of the month.

Now you have some options. What do you do with the extra? You could go out on the last day of the month to celebrate your discipline or roll it into the next month, but maybe you could use that money to practice generosity. It may not seem like much if it is a few dollars here and there, but it can add up. It is not ever about the size of the gift on our end, but what God can do with it on his end. Do you remember the story I mentioned earlier in John 6? There were thousands and thousands of people that needed to eat. A young boy had five loaves of barley bread and two fish. What good would that small gift do against such incredible need?

But he gave it to Jesus anyways. "If you can use the small gift I have to make a difference, it is all yours." And Jesus multiplied that gift and used it to feed all of them so that there were 12 baskets of leftovers. It is never about our efforts or our sacrifice. It is about what God can do when we release ourselves sacrificially back to Him.

That money could be used to buy a simple meal for someone who is homeless or to take a friend who is hurting out for a cup of coffer or even to pay for the cup of coffee of the person behind you in line. We can seek to be as generous as possible with all of the money God has entrusted to us, even the little bit left over at the end of the month. But do you know what is going to happen if you continue this habit of using cash? You are going to find that you are consistently spending less than you have allocated every month. When that happens, you can revise that category down and plan ahead every month to give that money from each category away towards bigger needs. That's what we who are a part of The Generosity Revolution are trying to do.

Before you argue using cash, try it for three months. I believe you will shocked at how much less you will spend without even really noticing. In the book, The Overspent American, Juliet Schot concluded that many Americans could cut their spending by 20% and not even really feel it. I believe using cash is one of the ways some of this reduction can happen with us, along with the other steps I am providing in this book. If we could spend 20% less, shouldn't we try anything we can for what is at stake, for the opportunity to give that lies in front of us?

I am aware of the challenges of using cash. The most difficult thing about using cash for day-to-day purchases is the "inconvenience" attached to it. In fact, it wouldn't surprise me if some of you reading this are convinced that it would be valuable, but are discounting putting it into practice because swiping a card is just easier. If that is the push back you are feeling, please don't take the easy road.

It would be so much easier if we didn't have to floss, right? Fast food restaurants exist on the hope that people will see swinging into a drive thru to spend more than they need to for their products. Did you know local gas stations actually make most of their profits on purchases in their convenience stores rather than on the sale of gasoline? What is easiest and most convenient is rarely the best option for us.

If we want to be as generous as possible with the money God has entrusted to us, then spending less on ourselves is going to be key. By getting in the habit of using cash whenever possible, we will spend less of God's money which will leave more money with which we can be generous.

HEART CHECK

One of the ways that you can help assure that you constantly think about The Generosity Revolution is to seek out encouragement from as many sources as possible to stay focused and motivated. I would encourage you to highlight encouraging sentences in this book and go back and set a day once a month where you can go back and read just those highlights. (This is a great practice whenever you encounter books that offer a radical departure from how you have been doing things. Our old habits can easily return if we don't feed the new habit.)

But don't stop there. Seek out other books and articles on the issues of stewardship and generosity. (You know, the ones you used to be tempted to skip!) Search for podcasts from your favorite communicators that deal with the use of money and resources. Find your local radio station that broadcasts Dave Ramsey's daily radio show and tune in regularly.

Why is this important? You are getting bombarded with the message of "spend, spend, spend" every day. Those messages are brought to you unsolicited many times a day—it could be the car that drives by, the commercial on your television, or the latest Apple™ product release. The only way you are going to stay focused on generosity is if you are fed the message of generosity regularly. Unfortunately, you are not going to get this message pumped into your head accidentally; this is going to have to be an intentional pursuit on your part.

My wife was interested in purchasing a camera from a friend. Her friend was selling two different cameras at different prices, and Angela was thinking the cheaper one was adequate for her needs. Wanting my wife to have the ultimate, I was encouraging her to spend the extra $100, justifying it with the fact that she would be able to use it for ministry, not just personal stuff.

That night, I picked up a book that had been sitting on my dresser in my "to read someday" pile by Jonathan Acuff entitled, *Gazelles, Baby Steps and 37 Other Things Dave Ramsey Taught Me about Debt*. I decided to pick it up and start reading. Those of you who have read it (I recommend you do) may remember, the very first chapter talked about three hobbies that we as Americans have a tendency to spend too much money on. Guess what one of three was? That's right. A camera. I laughed out loud and went and told Angela that I was okay with the cheaper one.

Here's my point: I consider myself serious about stewardship and have read tons of books and listened to many sermons. I am one of those guys that looks through podcasts and if there is one on money, I choose to listen to it first. (Okay, maybe there aren't any other guys like that. I am "that" guy.) But God still spoke to me and saved us from unnecessarily spending $100 because I read Acuff's book.

Do what it takes to keep growing in this. For you to stay focused on The Generosity Revolution, you are going to need to feed your desire to be generous. Let's face the truth. We already hear 'sermons' on money every day. The 'preacher' just isn't teaching us what the Bible says. We've got to feed our hearts and minds with encouragement towards what God has called us to be. If you catch yourself shying away from this topic, force yourself to face it so you can continue to grow.

Chapter Seven

STEP 6

ROUND DOWN WHEN SPENDING

AND ROUND UP WHEN GIVING

As we have already mentioned, the key to being a part of The Generosity Revolution is to spend less on me. The same is true for you. It takes intentional efforts to spend less on our kingdom so we are free to invest more in God's. People often ask, "How much am I supposed to give?" A better question is, "How little of God's money do we really need to keep?" Could you live on less than you currently are? For most of us the answer is "yes." From my experience, we could live on substantially less if we could change our habits.

As I mentioned in the introduction, being a part of The Generosity Revolution requires that we start thinking about generosity all of the time, every time we have the opportunity to spend money. Do you realize that every opportunity to spend is an opportunity to spend *less*? Have you ever thought of that?

What if every time you went to spend money, you tried to spend less? It doesn't have to be a lot less, but just a little less — every time. Maybe you could afford to spend more. That is not the point. Could you spend less? Start reminding yourself: Round down. Round down. Round down. Most of us have the habit of rounding up when we spend, and we're Americans so we do it in every category. We like to splurge every time we spend. What if we tried to reverse that mentality?

I am not trying to argue that we are not allowed to enjoy ourselves financially, but maybe we could spend a little less on the things that don't matter so more money is available for the things that really do. Instead of saying to yourself (or your spouse), "I'm sure we can afford to do a little more," when you face an opportunity to spend, start asking the question, "Is there any way we could spend a little less?" Let's round down when we are spending.

I will get to the large purchases a little later, but the biggest room for personal growth in establishing this habit is in the small things every day. Most of us can live on so much less. Think about the area of food. We literally eat so much of God's money in our culture!

What about going out to eat? When our family runs tight on money in a month, it is because we went out to eat too much. We have tried to get back to the point where going out to eat is something special, not part of our normal routine. Many of us could round down in the number of times we go out to eat. Could you? There is nothing wrong with going out to eat, but could you eat out less? It is significantly cheaper (and generally healthier) to eat at home which allows us more money with which to practice generosity.

When you do go out to eat, could you round down in the choice of restaurant? There is wide variety of restaurants at different price points. Could you round down? We often try to choose restaurants where we don't have to tip. You can now get quality food prepared fresh that isn't fast food where you don't have to tip. That saves you 20% off of your total cost each time. That is money that could be given away.

What about when you order? Could you round down in what you choose to order instead of rounding up? With the portion sizes at most restaurants, if you go out as a couple, could you choose to split a meal instead of getting two meals? Splitting meals is great for our wallets and our waistline. When deciding between a $12 meal and a $16 meal, or a $6 meal or a $9 meal, most of us are probably in the habit of rounding up. That is what we are used to doing. "I really feel like shrimp tonight," you might say. You always feel like shrimp! Maybe this time you could order the chicken. Round down so you have more to give away. Do you see how this Revolution can gain momentum in your own life?

Another option is to not eat dessert when you go out to eat for a meal. It is really bad for you and makes a huge difference in your bill. Or, if there is a restaurant that is known for their desserts (especially one that has dessert in the title!) maybe you could eat a small meal at home and then just go out for dessert. By the way, if you are just going out for dessert, I suggest doing so after the dinner rush has passed so you do not take away an opportunity for your server to get a meal-sized tip.

You could also drink water instead of soda or alcohol with your meal. It is significantly healthier and considerably cheaper. These are the types of daily decisions that those who are a part of The Generosity Revolution choose to make. Round down. Round down. Round down. You may want to start saying it quietly in your head as your peruse the menu!

Why is this so important? Because every time we go out to eat, we eat money that we could have given. What we ate really isn't going to matter to us tomorrow, at least not in a good way, right? Don't misunderstand. I am not saying we can never splurge. It is fine to enjoy a nice meal every once in a while. I'm saying we should not always splurge on us. Those who are part of The Generosity Revolution make the priority splurging on God and others.

When you go to a chain fast food restaurant, order off of the value menu. Let's face it. Nothing is really that good at these restaurants, so we may eat as little of God's money as possible! We'll go with other families that are our size and we will spend $10 and they will spend $25, and we both leave equally dissatisfied!

One of the choices that many of those who are a part of The Generosity Revolution have made is to make coffee at home. Have you ever totaled up how much you spend on coffee every month? Starbucks™ is in every prime location and churches aren't. Do you know why? Because people are willing to give without measure to

Starbucks by buying their coffee and people are holding back from the church.

Can I suggest a change that will allow you to be more generous? Take one month's worth of what you spend on coffee and buy a nice coffee pot. You can buy one that will grind and brew with a push of a button. Buy whole coffee beans from your favorite coffee shop and make it at home. Here's why this is so important. At the end of the year, are you going to look back and go, "I wish I would have been buying coffee at Starbucks all year?" No way. That isn't where true life is. But at the end of the year you will be glad that you were able to contribute more to those things that really do matter to you and for eternity.

I can't stress this enough. Here's why rounding down every time we spend is a no brainer to me and is so revolutionary. We're not going to miss the little stuff over time, and we can invest more in God's kingdom. God can use your rounding down in all of the little things to change people's lives. In fact, at The Pursuit we distributed business cards with The Generosity Revolution on the front and our church's website address on the back. (You can order some for your church on our website at www.thegenerosityrevolution.com. We encourage people to round down in what they spend on themselves and practice intentional acts of generosity (as opposed to random acts of kindness) with the money they would have spent on themselves. This isn't coming out of our giving; it is coming out of our entertainment money (and believe me, nothing is more fun than this).

Many have taken up the challenge and have decided to hit the drive thru and pay for the meal or beverage for the car behind them when they do go out and leave a GenRev card. Why not go out to eat less and give the server an incredible tip? Or maybe you look around the restaurant and ask God whom he would want you to bless? Hand your server a $20 bill with a card to give to the family or elderly couple that God put on your heart. You can visit our website or our facebook page to hear more ideas on what you can do with the money you save by rounding down. For those of you who are parents, this is a great demonstration of generosity to do with your children. I will share how this has impacted our family along with other encouragement for parents in Appendix B.

Movies is another category which I must mention when it comes to opportunities to round down. I don't know what it costs to see brand new movies at the theater in your town, but in Boise it is $10 for a ticket. If we choose to see a movie in the afternoon as a matinée, it is only $7.50. I am not opposed to occasionally going to see a movie as part of a special evening, but those of us who are looking to be as generous as possible should really consider the timing issue when we choose to watch movies. For a family of four, you will have $10 more to give if you simply choose to go to a movie on Saturday afternoon, rather than in the evening.

In Boise, we are blessed to have second run theaters that show movies for $2. If we can tolerate not being one of the first in our town to see a movie, our entire family could go for $14 (or $7 on Tuesdays when it is only $1). Our family of seven can go to see a movie when it first comes out at night for $70 or in the afternoon for $52.50. That is a lot of God's money! I could literally count on one hand the number of times our family has gone to see a first run movie, even as a matinée. We choose to wait until it comes out to the second run theater where the cost is $14 but even that has become more rare as we have tried to stretch ourselves in generosity. We mostly watch movies at home thanks to Redbox™. For the same movie (although admittedly less of an experience and requiring of some patience as we wait for the DVD to be released), we pay only $1. If you want to be as generous as possible, which should you spend to see a move, $70 or $1? Obvious choice indeed. Even for those of you who are single or married with no kids, the difference in cost for one or two movies can add up pretty quickly.

That covers some of the ideas for the small things, but what about the big stuff? Round down on the big stuff too. While we can save a few bucks rounding down on small things, and that can add up over time, we can save hundreds and in some cases thousands if we round down on the big stuff. When you decided what you wanted to spend to rent your last apartment, you probably decided what you would like to spend ahead of time. But if you are like most of us, you found that one that was perfect, even though it was higher than what you wanted to spend. Rather than passing on it, you rounded up and signed the lease. You decided it was worth spending a little more.

Think back to when you bought your house for those of you who have. I am guessing you probably started at a lower price point but then rounded up, by $5K, $10K, $50K or even $100K. Why not go the other way? If you can afford $250K, try to find a suitable house for $230K. You just saved $20K (actually significantly more after you take into account interest and property tax savings) that you can use for the Kingdom of God. What if you could afford a million dollar home? It doesn't mean you need to buy one. Think of how much more generous we could be as a nation!

What about when you bought your last car? You likely went in with a dollar value in mind and probably raised that amount when you got there. We know the reasons. It was the perfect color. It had all the options you wanted at a special package price. It was only $20 more per month for the additional "whatever" so you rounded up. What if you would have rounded down when you made all of these decisions? How much more generous could you have been?

When you buy your next car (with cash, right?), instead of raising the amount you are willing to spend, why not lower it? What if you have saved up $20,000 to buy a car, but then find a car for $15,000 that will meet your needs and put in a well in a third-world country with the other $5,000? Isn't that a better move? That is something those who are part of The Generosity Revolution would decide to do. Why? Six or seven years from now, you probably aren't even going to have that car, right? Even if you stretch it to ten or twelve years, that pales in comparison to the generations and generations that will have clean water because of your generosity. That is Revolutionary thinking!

And when you consider the eternal rewards, such rounding down is a no-brainer. Look at Matthew 10:42: Jesus says that, *"whoever in the name of a disciple gives to one of these little ones even a cup of cold water to drink, truly I say to you, he shall not lose his reward."* If even giving a cup of water to a child in need is rewarded, what will be the reward for putting in a well? What is the reward for giving thousands of children clean water until the return of Jesus? Wow.

One Pursuit family had saved up money to purchase a SUV they had been wanting for a few years. They finally had the money to pay cash and figured they could make a few thousand dollars selling their old minivan. When the time came for them to make the purchase, they discovered a minivan (not nearly as cool) that would meet their family's needs for $4000 less. After praying about it, they decided to round down and go with the lower-priced vehicle. That was a great move, but the real joy came when they went to sell their old minivan. Since they didn't spend the max on their new car, they realized they didn't need to get top dollar for their minivan. They ended up selling it for just $1000 to a family in the church they cared very much about that could not have afforded to pay the $3500 or so that the van was worth. I know they don't regret that decision now, but there is no way that they will regret it in eternity!

We have decided in our family that we are going to spend drastically less on cars in our lifetime than a typical American family with our income level. How? By spending less at the point of purchase by buying older cars that have a good reputation for reliability and then continuing to drive those cars until they need to be replaced instead of when we decide we are bored with the car. Many financial advisors have said that the cheapest car you can drive is the one you already own. This is obviously not true if you have overspent and have a significant car payment, but the advice is speaking against running out to buy a new car because the old car was costing so much in repairs.

I have spoken with people who went out and took payments on a new car because their old car was costing them too much in repairs in their mind. "Too much" for them meant a couple of hundred dollars this month when just three months ago they put in a couple of hundred more. It was just becoming to expensive to maintain in their mind so they went out and took on a $400 car payment every month in order to avoid having to pay $300 every few months. Does that seem strange to you? If we desire to be a part of The Generosity Revolution, we've got to start thinking of cars as what they really are. A horrible, but necessary for most, investment. Let's round down and spend less on our cars.

A typical American can literally spend hundreds of thousands of dollars less in their lifetime on cars than is normal in our culture. In the Good Sense Budget Course, a statistic was shared that although the average reliability for cars built today is ten years, people trade in their cars on average every four years. Do you know what that means over a lifetime? If you follow the average American's car-buying habits, you will drive 2.5 times more cars than you need to which means you will likely spend 2.5 times more money than you need to get you from point A to point B (which is ultimately the definition of what a car is for). Isn't that crazy? There is a better way.

We have drawn a line in the sand that we are going to buy the cheapest, reliable car we can that will adequately meet our family's needs. What line will you draw for your family? We are going to spend less on cars so that we have more to invest in God's work in the world. Why? Because cars really don't matter in comparison to changed lives. I refuse to be primarily a consumer. I want to be a part of The Generosity Revolution.

One last thought on rounding down before we move on. Think long term when you think about rounding down. Sometimes spending less up front will actually cost us more in the long run. Don't round down on quality on things that are long-term purchases. Pay attention to energy efficiency too. The cost to our environment is bigger and in many cases the financial cost can actually be greater too.

How different would your financial picture be if you started to round down every time you spend money?

I'd encourage you to stop and look back over the last couple of days at your purchases. Think back to your last major purchase. Did you round up?

If we are going to be as generous as possible with the money God has entrusted to us, then let's start rounding down every chance we get. Remind yourself that every opportunity you have to spend money is an opportunity to spend *less*. I am sitting at the Denver airport as I am typing this. My wife and I just split a piece of pizza When looking at the menu, we settled on the plain cheese piece of pizza for $3.30. We could have rounded up and ordered the pepperoni (with all of the extra calories and grease) or another more expensive version, but we decided to spend less. In and of itself, not a big deal. But when you add that to all of the other decisions to round down, it adds up pretty quickly! Start with your next purchase. Round down. Round down. Round down.

It is important to note that rounding down on spending does not necessarily make you more generous. I know some people that round down just to preserve their own resources. Perhaps you know someone like that who would fit the classification of a "tight wad." Unleash the habit of being more generous by beginning to round up whenever you have the opportunity to give. Instead of saying "I'm sure we can do more" when it comes to spending, I want to challenge you to start thinking that way when it comes to giving.

Have you ever found yourself debating over whether or not to leave four or five dollars for a tip? Pretty embarrassing if you think about it, huh? I can't tell you how many times I fought over a dollar to try to keep it for myself. Those who are part of The Generosity Revolution round up when it comes to opportunities to be generous. When you go out to eat, round down on the meal, but round up on the tip. When the percentage you have committed to give to your church is calculated, could you round up to the nearest five, ten or twenty-five dollars? Some of you with larger incomes, could you round up to the nearest fifty or hundred? Just like with rounding down in spending, rounding up in our giving establishes new habits that will eventually result in our hearts desiring to be more generous.

Heart Check

I want to encourage you to pay attention to where you tend to round up and where you tend to round down. It is an indicator of where your priorities currently are. In the book *Not a Fan* by Kyle Idleman, he points out that you can tell where people's hearts really are by how they prioritize spending, even though they claim that it is with Jesus. He asks a great question: "Why is it that when people are buying a house, they ask what the highest percentage of their monthly income it can safely be? But then when it comes to giving, people want to know if they have to tithe off of gross or if just off the net is okay?"

Ouch. That one's going to leave a mark, isn't it? Isn't it true that many of us scratch and fight about every dollar when it comes to giving, but we'll round up in our spending without even thinking about it? Why do we do that? Where are we really looking for satisfaction? There is no amount of rounding up in stuff (I don't care how much you round up) that will deliver the happiness that it promises long term. You'll only want something else. Something bigger. Something faster. Something newer. You will still be thirsty.

I wish we could all understand the futility, the pointlessness, of chasing after money and material things. It is a dead end street. There isn't an amount of stuff at which we will be satisfied. We will always want a little more. Ecclesiastes 5:10 states: "He who loves money will not be satisfied with money, nor he who loves wealth with his income; this also is vanity."

If we love stuff, we are never going to be able to buy everything we want, because as soon as we have it (whatever it is), we realize it doesn't satisfy and we will just want something else. Seeking satisfaction in stuff is a path made up of one disappointment after another. Only Jesus satisfies.

When tragedy strikes, it doesn't matter how big of house you have or what kind of a car you drive, does it? No one when they lose a loved one goes and looks at their savings account and finds peace, no matter how much is in there. Peace and hope is only found in Jesus. He is the living water. He is the only One who can quench your thirst. "Let them give thanks to the LORD for His lovingkindness, and for His wonders to the sons of men! For He has satisfied the thirsty soul, and the hungry soul He has filled with what is good" (Psalm 107:8-9).

We who have a relationship with our Creator don't have to try to get the most out of this life. We have everything we need. Let's reverse what we've been doing and try to give the most out of this life by being generous. Pay attention to where you desire to round up and where you are tempted to round down. It is a great way to test and see where our hearts really are.

GENEROSITY REVOLUTION

Chapter Eight

STEP 7

MAKE IT AUTOMATIC

There was a time when Christian parents would teach their kids that the first part of what you get (at least 10%) goes back to God. I was blessed to grow up with godly parents who taught me to give first before I did anything else with the money I received. My parents gave me my allowance in change so that it could be broken up into giving, saving, and spending. Like so many others who grew up when I did, I had parents who gave consistently and wanted their children to establish the habit of giving early. It worked for many of us. For those of us who grew up giving 10% or more, since we've been doing that for a couple of decades, it is automatic for us. But for so many of you who did not grow up with that kind of instruction and example, it is a constant struggle. It is a battle to remember to give and then to follow through with giving the amount that was decided ahead of time. If you have set out a goal to give consistently but have not been able to stick with it in the past, what do you do to establish a consistent habit?

The best thing for you to do would be to make it automatic. Go online and set up a recurring donation through your church's website if they have it or by using your bank's free bill pay. Most of us set up our 401K or IRA automatically, don't we? We set up our payment on our house, our investment in our real estate, as an automatic payment, don't we? Why? Because we don't want to miss a payment. That is a non-negotiable to us. It is too important to risk missing. Can I ask you something? Is the work of God any less important? His Kingdom should be the top priority, and contributing to it is the main reason why He entrusts money to us.

Many of us need to establish new habits with our giving and the hardest part about changing habits is the battle with self-control. Chip and Dan Heath, in a book entitled *Switch*, explain that self-control is an exhaustible resource. We've all experienced that, haven't we? The more we have to use self-control in an area, the more exhausting the battle becomes. It is harder and harder to fight it over time. If you put yourself in a situation where you are continuously having to exert self-control, it gets harder and harder to maintain it over time and in most cases we end up failing eventually.

You may be uncomfortable hearing this if you are familiar with the Bible because Galatians 5:22-23 explain that self-control is part of the fruit of the Spirit, the evidence that God is working in our life. If we were fully yielded to the Spirit on all occasions, we would never run out of self-control. But since we are broken and live in a world filled with temptation and distraction, we should not intentionally put ourselves in a position to test our self-control when we have demonstrated a lack of it in our previous experience. If you are a guy that struggles with lust, I would not encourage you to go spend extra time at a beach surrounded by bikini-clad sunbathers to work on your self-control with your eyes. If you are a teenager trying to exhibit self-control in the physical arena, don't go sit in the backseat of a car with your girlfriend or boyfriend in isolated places. Don't be at each other's homes when no one else is around. Do you remember Paul's instruction in 1 Corinthians 6:18, which is the same example that Joseph gave us when he faced the temptation from Potiphar's wife in Genesis 39? Run! Flee from it. Don't stick around to see how strong you are. If you are struggling to gain self-control with your diet, do you leave cookies on the counter and stock the freezer with ice cream just to practice self-control? I hope not.

If you are a guy that struggles with lust, stay away from the beach until you have established the habit of self-control. If you are a young person who wants to stay pure, avoid putting yourself in positions where your self-control will be pushed to the limit. If you are trying to lose weight, don't keep junk food in your kitchen (or in your bedroom!). And if you struggle with remembering to give or you just seem to spend all of your money before Sunday rolls around, make it automatic.

Wouldn't it be nice if we could automatically control our tongue? Or our eyes? Can you imagine if we could make a "decision" and then no longer slip in any other area? We would all love that. Unfortunately, we can't go to a website, fill in a few fields, and click return to escape the battle of self-control with anger or alcohol or our tongues. But we can do that with giving. Save the self-control battles for other areas where you don't have a choice. Use the virtue of self-control to keep you out of a situation where you may be tempted instead of choosing to test it by putting yourself in the situation where you have previously collapsed under the pressure.

Make it automatic. You have hopefully already decided the amount you plan to give on your spending plan. Take that amount and break it into two payments and schedule your donations to come out of your account the day after your payday. For those of you with variable incomes or want to make it a deliberate act of giving when you get paid instead of a deliberate act of scheduling it, set an appointment in your calendar to remind you to give as soon as you get paid. With the online option, you can give to God any day of the week just like you can spend any day of the week. Or if you give the old-fashioned way, write your check and make sure that you remember to bring it. If you are going to miss a Sunday, commit to mailing in your investment.

One of the most discouraging things in observing giving in the church today is that giving consistently drops in the summer. People apparently prioritize spending on vacations over giving to support their local church. If we would all make it automatic, our churches would have a more steady income instead of the seasonal peaks and valleys that make management of the church finances more challenging than they need to be.

Speaking of challenges, would you let me challenge those of you who are pushing back on the idea of making it automatic because it doesn't sound as spiritual for a moment? Before you decide not to, would you look back over your checkbook for the last year and make sure you did not miss any gifts? I can tell you from being in the ministry for a while, most people miss a donation or two (or more) throughout the year. If you have missed some of your giving, then perhaps you should make it automatic. We have to consider that Satan our enemy does not like what the church accomplishes, and he would love to convince you and others that you shouldn't make your giving automatic if it is going to hurt the church. If your decision to not make it automatic is hurting your local church or the child you support monthly, then that cannot be the best decision. Failing to give what God is calling us to give is a significant issue.

In Malachi 3, God says these words through His prophet to the people of Israel. "Will a man rob God? Yet you are robbing Me! But you say, 'How have we robbed You?' In tithes and offerings" (Malachi 3:8). This is an incredible statement. God tells the people that they are stealing from Him. By not giving Him what He deserved, they were robbing God.

Let me ask you something: If you heard that someone broke into your home church and stole cash out of their safe, how would you feel about that person? I'm not talking about the good Christian answer of, "I'd pray for His soul." I'm talking about how you really would feel. You'd probably think something like this: "What? What kind of a person would steal from a church?" But do you know what this passage shows us? In God's eyes, when we don't give what God is calling us to give, we are stealing from Him. If you are not giving what you are called to give to your church, it is the same thing as breaking into their safe and stealing money from it.

Obviously we don't see it that way, and it would not surprise me if there was some discomfort in hearing it and a feeling inside of you to just dismiss it, but stay with me. The people of Israel did not see it as stealing either and that's why their anticipated response by the prophet Malachi was, "How have we robbed you?" Just because we don't view it as stealing does not mean that it is not stealing.

Think of it this way. When you have something that is rightfully someone else's and you don't return it to them, is that stealing? Of course it is. If I found a wallet with a $100 bill in it and quickly discovered (unfortunately for me!) that it had a driver's license in it so I knew to whom the money belonged, if I did not return it to them that would be considered what? Stealing, right? I would be keeping what I clearly knew belonged to someone else. When we don't return to God the portion He calls us to give, it is stealing. We have got to stop robbing God by stealing from His church. Our heart for God is not going to increase if we are continually robbing Him. Remember Chapter 1? Our hearts are still going to be tethered. It isn't where we intend to put our treasure that pulls our hearts; it is where we actually put our treasure. If you struggle to follow through, make it automatic.

I also want to remind you that God is not the only person we're robbing when we don't give as He has called us to give. We also rob those closest to us. Malachi 3:9 tells us that the nation of Israel was cursed because of how they were robbing Him. He tells them that their sin was impacting their families, their wives and children. God is not going to bless people who are stealing from Him. If you catch an employee stealing from your company, do you promote them? Of course not. They were now struggling financially because God was withholding His financial blessing from them.

I want to encourage you to make the commitment to give what God is calling you to give by making it automatic. God will bless you for doing so. You can have confidence in His promises. In fact, God says you can test Him by giving what He is calling you to give to see if He really will provide. The only place the Bible invites us to test God is in giving. Look at Malachi 3:10-12:

" 'And test Me now in this,' says the Lord of hosts, 'if I will not open for you the windows of heaven and pour out for you a blessing until it overflows. Then I will rebuke the devourer for you, so that it will not destroy the fruits of the ground; nor will your vine in the field cast its grapes,' says the Lord of hosts. 'All the nations will call you blessed, for* *you shall be a delightful land,' says the Lord of hosts.*"

Let's commit to giving what is rightfully God's back to Him every time we get paid. There is no better way to solidify that commitment than to make it automatic.

HEART CHECK

Although I believe that we should make it automatic when we can when it comes to how we give, I don't believe we should assume that it is automatic as to where we should give all of our resources.

I absolutely believe that God can and does call individuals to minister to specific groups of people. He lays burdens on our hearts to care for and reach out to a particular race, ethnic group or pocket of society. But I wonder if any of us would ever use the absence of a "call" to be generous with a particular group or even an individual as a cover up for some type of prejudice we possess?

Let me ask the questions another way. Is there any group of people that you would not be excited about blessing with your resources? Is there an ethnic group that you would not consider supporting? What about your attitude towards the homeless? Ask God to reveal if there is any lack of love for any of His children and look for other areas to practice generosity.

The Generosity Revolution isn't limited to money. Some of you maybe don't have any income to give right now. God does not expect any of us to give what we do not have. He expects us to give out of what we do have. Isn't that refreshing? Can you be generous with your time? Can you volunteer in a community organization? Are you using your gifts with your listening ear to someone who is hurting? You can do things like let someone go in front of you in line at the grocery store when they just have a few items or let the car trying to merge go in front of you. Remember, those who are a part of a revolution think about it all of the time. Every day is an opportunity to practice generosity, even if money is not involved in the transaction.

You can be generous by inviting people into your home. Hospitality is a precious gift that can be shared with others. If God has blessed us with a home, we are invited to use it to bless others. But, perhaps when we ask ourselves, "Whom do we want to have over for dinner," we aren't actually practicing generosity. If the motivation for having someone over is that we enjoy their company and that it would be an equal blessing to us, then we need to be honest about our motivation.

Maybe a better questions is, "Whom should we have over for dinner?" To whom would it be the biggest blessing? To whom would it be a genuine act of generosity? Is there someone that doesn't normally get invited over, maybe because they are socially awkward or maybe even annoying? Maybe their kids are a little out of control? Perhaps that is exactly whom you should invite if you are trying to be a part of The Generosity Revolution. (By the way, if a bunch of your friends read this book and all of a sudden they start inviting you over for dinner, don't take it personally. I am sure it is just a coincidence.) Look at these words Jesus said in Luke 14, which somehow have failed to catch our attention as a culture:

"And He also went on to say to the one who had invited Him, "When you give a luncheon or a dinner, do not invite your friends or your brothers or your relatives or rich neighbors, otherwise they may also invite you in return and that will be your repayment. But when you give a reception, invite the poor, the crippled, the lame, the blind, and you will be blessed, since they do not have the means to repay you; for you will be repaid at the resurrection of the righteous" (Luke 14:12-15, NASB).

Jesus isn't saying we should never invite people we would enjoy. Relationships that fill us are a valid and necessary joy in life, but just don't call it generosity. Your only reward for inviting people you enjoy over for dinner is the enjoyment you gain from spending that time.

I can remember getting struck with this passage years ago. We were practicing what we thought was generosity when we would take a different family out for pizza every once in a while after church. We realized that we were really only enjoying our time with friends we already had who didn't really need the financial help that would probably buy us lunch someday in return. Oops. So we asked the question, "Whom should we take out to lunch?"

God brought a couple to mind immediately in our church. They were people with whom we would not normally hang out. I had known the wife since I was a kid and always knew there was something wrong mentally, but I never knew what it was. We were all pleasantly surprised when she started dating someone and eventually they got married. They had a couple of kids that had physical and mental challenges. You may be thinking, "I know someone like that, but there's no way we could have them over or take them out to dinner." I tried to tell God the same thing. What would they think? Out of the blue, we are just supposed to go up and tell them we'd like to go out to lunch? But that's exactly what we did.

I'm not going to lie. It was pretty awkward at first. We just asked them about their children's physical problems and how they were handling all of it. And then it happened. You see, the wife had epilepsy, and she started going into a small seizure. It was nothing violent, but her mind locked up and she started trembling. Her husband lovingly held her hand and just kept whispering to her. "I'm here. I love you. You are going to be okay. It will pass in just a minute." Wow. What a precious moment. My heart broke. I could not stop the tears from welling up in my eyes.

I thought I was doing something that would bless them, but instead God was blessing me. That is the way generosity works. I am sure they didn't think too much of the lunch although I know they appreciated it, and they probably didn't remember it down the road. But remembering that moment and seeing a husband with limited mental capacity pour out perfect love for his wife that he cherished still brings tears to my eyes fifteen years later.

My guess is that by now you probably have someone in mind and you are already trying to talk you and God out of the need to do so. You are a part of The Generosity Revolution. Give to those who do not have the means to repay you, from which you expect nothing in return, and you will be rewarded by Jesus.

Chapter Nine

STEP 8

CHANGE HOW YOU PRAY

For which do you pray for more often: more content-ment or more money? We know that more money will not necessarily result in us being more generous, but more contentment definitely will. Why? Because in your mind you will already have enough with what you currently have under your stewardship. Once you are content with what you have, when new money comes in, your thoughts are free to move outside of your own needs and desires as you consider what to do with it. When we don't have the list in our head of all of the things we can't wait to buy for ourselves, our attention is free to be directed outside of our kingdom and is able to focus on God's.

In the great DVD series by Andy Stanley entitled "Balanced," he talks about the importance of what we do with the "extra" that we have. It is rare that I speak with people who truly believe that they have any "extra" even though we westerners are the richest Christians in history. Somehow we just don't see it that way. In fact, you probably ask for "more" quite often. Perhaps we are praying for "more" of the wrong thing. Let's change how we pray and start asking for more contentment. How actively are you pursuing contentment? In our consumeristic culture, with all of the need that surrounds us, I believe this should be near the top of our prayer list for ourselves and those who are close to us. In Hebrews 13:5, it is written, "Make sure that your character is free from the love of money, being content with what you have; for He Himself has said, "I WILL NEVER DESERT YOU, NOR WILL I EVER FORSAKE YOU." Are you making sure you are free from the love of money? I think somehow most of us have ignored that we should be actively pursuing contentment, rather than pursuing and praying for more money. More money and stuff without giving can actually pull us away from God, while more contentment frees us to live more fully for Him. More contentment is what will allow us to be more generous. To be a part of The Generosity Revolution, we've got to change how we pray.

I think there is a specific reason why God has not given many of us more money. As a parent, do you always say yes when your kids ask you for something? I remember when my son used to ask for candy at breakfast virtually every day. I knew it would be harmful so I did not answer his request with a "yes" (at least most of the time). God will hold back giving us material things that we ask for if it is not good for us to have more. God knows that more money in the hands of those who mismanage it will only be more mismanaged money. Think about it. If your heart is tethered because you aren't giving what you should, to give you more would just put you in further bondage.

Some of us who want to be generous genuinely believe that if we made more, we would give a higher percentage. We frequently believe that we need more money in order to be able to give more. The reality is that most of us would not give more if we had more. While you may be able to give more in actual dollars if your income went up, generosity is not about the amount you give, but the amount of sacrifice that the gift represents. The more Christians make in America, the less they tend to give as a percentage. Christians aren't giving as they prosper according to scripture, but inversely to how they prosper. It is backwards. How could this be? Consider these survey results from *The Overspent American*. Juliet Schot conducted a telemarketing survey that revealed some disturbing results. The survey asked participants if they would be satisfied with their income if they had an increase that was less than 20%.

Among those making $30,000 a year or less, 81% said they needed to make less than 20% more to be satisfied. Among those making $75K a year or more, only 40% said they needed to make less than 20% more to be satisfied. Isn't that amazing? Probably not what you'd expect. Apparently the answer to being satisfied with our income is not having more income. The more we make, the more we believe that a little bit more will not be enough. This survey illustrates the truth found in Ecclesiastes 5:10. "Whoever loves money never has enough; whoever loves wealth is never satisfied with their income." Maybe it is not good for you to have more. The problem with getting more money is that greed can set in when you get more money.

I want to drill down on this a little bit. It is the sin of greed that is actually tethering our hearts if they are tethered to the world. What is greed? The desire for more than what you already have. It has become so culturally acceptable to us as Christians to have these desires, that it doesn't even sound like a sin, does it? Of course we want more, right? We're supposed to want a bigger house than we have and a newer car than we have and more toys than we have, right? No. Not as followers of Jesus. We are to be satisfied with what we have because we are satisfied with Him.

Let's look at what Jesus says about greed in Luke 12:15: "Beware, and be on your guard against every form of greed; for not even when one has an abundance does his life consist of his possessions.' " I may be going out on a limb here, but I would guess that very few of us ever put any effort or thought into guarding against greed. Very few of us make intentional efforts to stop our minds from wandering towards newer and shinier and more and instead point ourselves back to gratitude for what we already have. Protection from greed doesn't make our prayer lists. It really should.

How dangerous is the love of money in believers? Incredibly dangerous. I think many of us are in incredible danger spiritually. What if we think we are doing okay, but Satan is luring us away? Some of you may think I am exaggerating. That I am paranoid. Maybe I am paranoid. I think a little paranoia is healthy. But I am not exaggerating. Look at 1 Timothy 6:10. "For the love of money is a root of all sorts of evil, and some by longing for it have wandered away from the faith and pierced themselves with many griefs."

Paul describes in his day that people had wandered away from that faith that they at one time professed because they wanted more money. Could that happen today? I think with the luxuries and toys that we have available to us, we could expect that it is even a greater issue in our day. It could happen to any one of us if we are not careful. Have you turned away from money and stuff or are you still tethered? Is your heart still in danger?

But our love of money also deeply impacts those around us. I was reading about the history of DR Congo from where we recently adopted two toddlers, Malachi and Mercy. The book was about slave trade that took place there in the late 1800s and early 1900s. Did you know what floored me about it above all else in these gruesome stories? Christians were participating in it. Missionaries were involved. The same was true here in America during the time when slavery was legal. Many of the people trading and owning slaves were professing Christians. People who have the same Bible that we do, that tells us that God loves all the nations and we are to love our neighbor as ourselves owned slaves, holding them against their will and treating them as if they were less than human because of the color of their skin.

How could they be so blind? How could they go to church on Sundays and sing to God and then go home to humans for whom Jesus died, many of whom were their brothers and sisters in Christ, as if they were property? What blinded them? Do you know? You may have never thought of it, but it was the love of money. They saw an opportunity to gain money. It was all financial. Their eyes were blinded by greed.

No matter what our income level and what we possess, we are all to guard against greed. We need to change how we pray and ask for more contentment instead of asking for more money. Unless something changes in our hearts first, the more money we make, the smaller percentage we will give. We will become less generous if we get more. Why? We like to think that the more we have, the more satisfied we will be. But the truth is, the more we have, the more dissatisfied we become. Our hearts become more tethered.

Check out this downward spiral into which many of us have fallen. Whenever we buy more stuff beyond our needs, our heart becomes a little more tethered to the world, which makes us want more stuff. What happens when we get more stuff? Greed takes a greater hold of us, which makes us want more stuff, so we buy more, which makes our heart even more tethered and down and down we go. God wants us to have the opposite of greed in our hearts which is contentment. Contentment drives greed away. They can't coexist. Do you know what the best greed repellent is? Giving. Giving is first and foremost about our hearts being drawn towards

God. That is why the first thing we need to do when we receive income is give God His portion. If we keep all of the money for ourselves, it grabs hold of us.

To those of us who are His followers, Jesus instructs us that we ought to be actively trying to guard our hearts and minds from wanting more. If where our treasure is, there our heart will be also, we ought to be cautious when we spend to guard against greed. Before we spend our extra, we should ask the question, "Is what I am going to buy going to compete with the attention of my heart?" Remember, if we spend it we can't give it.

However, when we give there is a spiral upward which I pray will be the pattern of all of us who desire to be a part of The Generosity Revolution. You see, when we give our heart becomes more for God which builds contentment in our hearts. This greater contentment allows us to decide against buying some of the extras we don't need. When we spend less, it allows us to give more which draws our heart more towards God, which of course makes us more content and up and up and up we go. Wouldn't that be amazing if that became your story of transformation?

Let's start diligently praying for more contentment. Let's start begging God for more of it in our hearts, that He would bless us abundantly... with contentment!

Contentment is always good for you. Pray faithfully for contentment and God will answer it. He will not withhold from us what is good. In 1 Timothy 6:8, the apostle Paul writes, "If we have food and covering, with these we shall be content." We have a lot more than that, don't we? And yet we still want more.

Jesus warns us to not buy the lie that life and happiness is found in stuff. We can chase it all, but it will never satisfy. King Solomon was the wealthiest man alive, and he said it was all meaningless. The apostle Paul lost everything but was okay, because he explained that he had learned to be content. We need to pray for more contentment. I want to offer you a "get-rich-quick" opportunity. You can be instantly rich. We think people are rich if they have the money to buy whatever they really want to buy. That can be true of you in one of two ways: either you win the lottery so you have a seemingly unlimited supply to buy what you want (which the odds indicate that is likely not going to happen to you) or you can finally be content what you have. If we are truly content, we'll have all the money we need to buy everything we want because we'll already have everything we want.

What do you have enough of? Honestly. Do you have enough square feet? Enough horsepower? Enough inches of screen real estate on your TV? Enough pairs of shoes? Enough recreational toys? Enough bulk that you can stop buying supplements? Enough ink on your body? Enough gold and diamonds? Enough video games? Enough DVDs that you never watch? Enough paintings around your house? Enough Christmas decorations? What do you finally have enough of?

I am not saying any of these things are wrong for us to enjoy. They are just not nearly as important as the work of God in the world. The pursuit of any of them can be a trap that can tether our hearts. For our churches and ministries to have all that they need to fulfill their mission, we just need to all get to the point where we want people to know Jesus more than we want the bigger house, the newer car, or the latest Apple product.

The time has come for us to be done with the pursuit of more, at least more money and stuff. Let's pursue contentment. If we want to be as generous as possible with the money God has entrusted to us, we need to change how we pray and start asking for more contentment instead of more money.

HEART CHECK

How do we know that we are becoming content? I think we can tell by what we say to ourselves and the other decision-makers when we are considering spending. When our hearts are discontent and we are focused on material things, we are going catch ourselves justifying purchases. We'll say to ourselves and those around us who are watching, "We can afford that. I think we are okay to buy that." My dad taught me that just because I could afford to do something, that did not necessarily make it right. Maybe there was a better use of that money.

When our heart is free from the love of money and stuff, when we are content, we are going to find ourselves saying to ourselves and those around us, "We don't really need that. Yeah, we could afford it, but do we really need it?" And we are going to walk away from more opportunities to spend.

We've seen contentment grow in our lives as we have become more and more focused on generosity. Our love for stuff is disappearing. For example, my wife and I have finally stopped taking an empty suitcase with us on vacation. We literally used to plan ahead and take an empty suitcase with us on trips because we'd always seem to end up at outlet malls and would find so many great deals on things we didn't really need, but we bought them anyways. We know the money we save when we practice contentment and pass on a purchase we could have made, but we can't know the degree to which God is going to work in our hearts as we practice contentment. I want to share one story of how God blessed us when we finally decided we had enough in one category. I hope it encourages you.

As a young guy, I loved stereo systems (just like every other guy I knew). Being in a dorm with other guys only fed this desire for louder. I remember getting my first receiver with surround sound. It was amazing. You could actually hear sound behind you! I knew it couldn't get any better. But then it did. Dolby Pro Logic was the next thing. I had to have it. And of course, now I had to buy another speaker for the center channel. (Has anyone else noticed that every upgrade seems to require additional speakers? It is almost as if the electronics companies are out to try to get us to spend more money.)

I think to ease the guilt of buying a new receiver that I didn't need, I decided to give away my old receiver to a friend. The new Pro-logic receiver was amazing, until the next year or so when Dolby Digital came out. Now I had to have that. (Does this sound familiar to any of you? If you guys don't remember, I'm sure your wives do!)

I went and got a new receiver, actually it was refurbished because I wanted to round down, from a quality manufacturer. Just like in the previous case, it did not take long for it to be outdated. It took about one year, actually. Then it finally struck me. When is this going to end? If I buy the latest and greatest, within a year, it won't satisfy me either. I made a commitment that I was going to be content with what I had. I decided I would not replace our electronics toys until they needed to be replaced, as in, stopped working. What started as a commitment to better stewardship and contentment in electronics began to extend into other areas as well.

I have to tell you how God rewarded our commitment. I had a young lady at our church that wanted to purchase a new stereo system for her home. She had the money so she invited me to shop for her system. Although I couldn't buy new stuff for me, I could enjoy buying for someone else. I picked out the receiver I would have purchased for me, which at that time was the latest and greatest.

Fast forward a few months. Our receiver, which was now more than five years old (beyond obsolete in electronics world!), started shutting off when it warmed up after being on for about fifteen minutes. The great thing about a commitment to waiting until things are broken before you replace them is you actually are excited when things break! (No, I did not pour water on it or anything. That would be cheating.)

But something had happened to me. I had become so content with the receiver that I actually did not want to spend several hundred dollars to replace it, because that would have reduced our ability to be generous. We decided that we would see what it would cost to get it repaired, and then only replace it if the cost to repair it did not make sense in comparison to what the receiver was actually worth.

The repair shop informed me that they were able to determine what was causing the unit to shut off, but that they had discovered another problem with the receiver that I did not even notice. Where it began to get interesting was that they told me that they were having trouble locating the part. They informed me that it was required by law that manufacturers make parts available to older electronics so they could not be accused of forcing people to purchase new equipment.

You aren't going to believe what happened next. A few days later I received a phone call from the manufacturer telling me that they no longer had that part available so they would be sending me a replacement receiver. Guess what receiver they sent as a replacement? Yep, the exact same unit I had just purchased for the friend! God has a way of rewarding our faithfulness.

Chapter Ten

STEP 9

STEP IT UP

Even in the tightest budgets, when there is an unplanned increase in a monthly expense, we figure out a way to make it work. We'll pull something from one category and cut back on another in order to compensate for the increase. What happens in our households when gas prices suddenly shoot up? We make the adjustment. If we have an unexpected medical bill, we figure out how to make it work, right?

Think back to the last time you bought a car with payments or took on some other debt (which hopefully you are committed to avoiding in the future). My guess is that you started out with a certain price in mind but then had the opportunity to round up (which we discussed in Chapter 7). Why were you willing to spend more? As you were considering the purchase, you probably justified how you could afford to take on the increase in this new payment by pulling it from other things. You said to yourself (and maybe your spouse), "If we cut a little bit here... If we didn't spend as much there... we could make it work." If we can survive increases in other categories, whether those increases are forced on us or we willingly take them on, why not try that with giving? Why not just try increasing the amount that you give and then force yourself to come up with the money by cutting from other categories?

I believe that every one of us could give away a higher percentage of our income than we currently are right away. Some of you reading this could give a substantially higher percentage, especially if you faithfully applied all of the principles in this book. Could you go up 3, 5 or 8% more? Some of your budgets may be pretty tight. Could you go up just 1 or 2%? Why not step it up?

How long have you been giving the percentage you currently are? Instead of just saying someday you'd like to give more, which is maybe why you bought this book, why not just do it now? Why not just step it up? If you were raised in the church and you've been giving 10% as long as you can remember, good job. Why not go to 12 or 15%? If you've previously stretched yourself to 15% and now that has become easy, why not go to 17 or 18%? For those of you who have been more or less "tipping" God at 2.5% or less (which is what the average American "Christian" gives), why not go to 5%? Or maybe just go to 10% and see what happens? I know it is scary to do that, but God will take care of you.

What are you afraid will happen if you increase your percentage? Do you honestly believe that God will fail you? I can tell you from the promises in His word, from personal experience, and from observation of others who have increased the percentage they give, God will bless your faithfulness and will add to your capacity to give.

Look at Paul's instruction in dealing with generosity. "Now this I say, he who sows sparingly will also reap sparingly, and he who sows bountifully will also reap bountifully" (2 Corinthians 9:6). If you want God to bless you financially, give faithfully and generously. God accepts full responsibility for providing for those who faithfully manage His resources and give generously to support His work in the world. When someone steps it up, God supplies. I have seen it over and over again. How we use our extra now impacts how much extra God will give us in the future.

Paul goes on to explain, "Each one must do just as he has purposed in his heart, not grudgingly or under compulsion, for God loves a cheerful giver. And God is able to make all grace abound to you, so that always having all sufficiency in everything, you may have an abundance for every good deed" (2 Corinthians 9:7-8). It clearly states that if we are generous, we will have an abundance. More importantly, it explains the purpose for which we are given that abundance. Did you notice that? We get an abundance "for every good deed." He does not promise more so that we can buy everything we want. Paul continues the thought with this: "Now He who supplies seed to the sower and bread for food will supply and multiply your seed for sowing and increase the harvest of your righteousness; you will be enriched in everything for all liberality, which through us is producing thanksgiving to God" (2 Corinthians 9:10-11). He will multiply our seed, our resources, for what purpose? For sowing, not spending. We will be enriched for all liberality, so that we can be even more generous.

I need to clarify that this is not the prosperity gospel that is so prevalent in today's American churches. The prosperity gospel teaches that if you give to God, He promises that He will make you financially rich on this earth. It is amazing that many are blinded to the problems with dangling a carrot of wealth out in front of Christians to encourage them to give. Who is the true master at that point? If we give to God to get rich, are we really serving God or are we serving money? If we give to God in order to get money, then really we are just worshiping money and stuff and using God to try to get more of what we really love. God knows our hearts. He knows why we are giving.

I would not be surprised if some of you are looking at your own financial situation right now and you are doing quite well and you don't give. You may be thinking, "I don't give much and God's blessed me with plenty." Have you ever considered that maybe your financial abundance isn't the blessing of God? Maybe it is the work of Satan. Perhaps he is giving you abundance because he knows you will keep it all for yourself and your heart will be even more tethered. In fact, for those of you who are not yet followers, it can be incredibly difficult if you are well-off to you coming to faith in Jesus.

Jesus said it is nearly impossible for a rich person to become a follower of God. Why? Because they think they have everything. "Who needs God? I don't need the Holy Spirit to comfort me, I can buy comfort. I don't need God's wisdom, I've got a great education." But money doesn't go to eternity with you. Don't be fooled. Money and stuff was never supposed to be worshiped. Jesus alone is the one for whom we should live.

For those of us who desire to please Him, when we step up our giving for His sake, the Bible is clear that we will be blessed with more. If we give to God or others as an expression of our love for God and others, God will provide more with which we will be able to continue to be generous. In other words, if you want to be more generous, step it up with what you already have. God will make sure to supply so that you can be even more generous.

Sometimes he supplies through raises or a promotion. Sometimes it is extra money that comes in that you didn't expect. It can be a string of months without anything breaking down. God can stretch our dollars further. We've seen God do all of those things in our lives, but I'll tell you what He has done the most for us as we have stepped up our percentage. God has just taken away our love for stuff. I still enjoy things, don't get me wrong, but I don't crave them. I don't long for stuff I don't have. I have seen my heart for things diminish as our percentage has moved up. There has been a direct correlation in our lives. Giving drives away greed.

If you have been faithfully giving, you have already experienced the reality of God's faithfulness in your life. God has not left you without provision. You may not be rich, but you have enough. Could you stretch a little and step it up? If God has given you enough to give at the level at which you currently give, why not increase the percentage, trusting that He will supply then too? God will make sure that we can continue being a part of The Generosity Revolution.

As you think of stepping it up, there is no doubt some tension as to if you should do so now and to what kind of increase you should step up. I am sure there is part of you that would be excited about giving more... at least at first. But then what happens? You start to think of all of the things you won't be able to buy, or maybe the places you won't be able to go, and you decide that maybe you should delay an increase in order to do a little bit more for yourself.

This would be a great time to address the question, "How much am I supposed to give to God?" How do we know when we are giving the appropriate percentage? As we have already seen in Chapter 2, we are to surrender ownership of all of our money when we come to faith in Jesus, but God allows us to maintain management of it. How do we determine the amount we are called to give? It would be nice if there were a flat percentage for all of us or even a table, like the government provides for our taxes, that existed for giving. We could just find our income on the axis that shows the income range and move across the page and find the column that shows how many dependents we have, and the bracket would just show us what percentage God is calling us to give. Unfortunately it is not that simple.

There are some who teach that the tithe belongs to God and He requires it of us, and the 90% left over is completely at our discretion, as if it is primarily intended for us to consume but can also be given if we choose to do so. The New Testament never even hints that God would only ask 10% of us. It is all His and He may require more of it back than 10%. In fact even the Old Testament teaches that 10% may not be enough to be doing what God requires.

Look at verse 8 from Malachi 3 one more time. This passage is most frequently quoted with the challenge to tithe (give a full 10% of your income) to God. I want to ask you to read it carefully and see if you can discover anything new that you did not see before. "Will a man rob God? Yet you are robbing Me! But you say, 'How have we robbed You?' In tithes and offerings." Do you notice anything unusual in that verse that maybe you didn't ever see before? I confess that I had never observed what was pointed out to me in *The Treasure Principle* by Bruce Wilkinson.

God says they were robbing Him in tithes *and* offerings. The tithe was required, but offerings were "voluntary." They were robbing God by not giving what was voluntary, over and above what was clearly required. How could that be? How could they be robbing Him with what He did not clearly call them to give? If God gives us extra, it is implied that we'll give more than the minimum. That's why He is giving us extra.

If you tithe, you could be tithing faithfully, giving 10% of your gross (not net) income to your local church, just as you have been taught and still be robbing God. "But I thought 'offerings' were voluntary?" you might protest. They are, but that does not mean they are not expected. We have already looked at the fact that God has given you a surplus so that you can give more of it back.

So if there is no table at which we could look, and 10% is not enough for everyone, how much are we supposed to give to not be robbing God? Why didn't God tell the Israelites the percentage they were supposed to give to not be robbing Him? Probably because they did not ever ask. God will give us wisdom if we ask. Have you asked God what He wants you to give? Have you laid all of your resources on the table and said, "God, how much do you want me to give to Your church where I attend? How much do I give to other ministries that are doing your work in the world?" I believe there is a percentage that God expects each of us to give that is specific to us, as He has prospered us (1 Corinthians 16:2).

I want to talk to those of you who faithfully give a percentage of your income for just a minute. When was the last time you asked God if He wanted that percentage to increase? You are doing well by giving something, perhaps even a good percentage, don't get me wrong. But if you have been giving faithfully, God has blessed you so you could give even more. Are you regularly asking Him if He is calling you to give more? We should always be listening for His voice.

On October 17, 2010, God called us clearly to adopt a boy, a little brother for our only son Micah who was four at the time. We believed, although we were not sure at the time, that we were to adopt from Africa. From that point on, we were committed to adopt a little preschool-aged boy, although challenges in our personal lives pushed it further into the future than we originally assumed. Sometimes God clearly calls us to do something, but the timing isn't right just yet. He is simply preparing us for that which He is calling us to do in the future. God called me to "someday go somewhere where I don't know anyone and start a church" back in 1996. It wasn't until May of 2003 that He told me it was time and where it was to be. God had more work in me, more that I was to learn, before it was time to act on that call so he could work through me.

Similarly, it wasn't until eighteen months after our clear call that we were to adopt, in March of 2012, that I went to Uganda. As part of the trip, I was able to visit two different orphanages. Before I left for the trip, we believed that God was calling us to move forward with the adoption and literally went into both orphanages wondering if one of the young boys I was to meet was the one that God had created to by my son. It was an amazing feeling to walk into both with anticipation to see if there was going to be an instant connection, a whisper from God saying, "That one. He's the one."

God didn't identify clearly at either orphanage that one of them was my son. In fact, through that visit, I felt that God was not telling us to adopt from Uganda, but rather from the DR Congo, where two other families in our church had adopted. But God did say something else to me while I was visiting the orphanages. His message was clear. We were to adopt a boy *and* a girl.

We are so blessed today to not just have Malachi as our son but to have Mercy as our daughter. Her smile has touched everyone who has seen it. Let me ask you something? What if we would have not kept listening? What if we had heard only the first command and then stopped listening to God? What if we thought that the first time we heard from God was His final answer? We wouldn't have our precious Mercy.

I'm glad we kept listening. Are you still listening for what God is calling you to do? There's an important question to address for us to understand why we still need to listen, why maybe His first call to us was not His ultimate call. If God wanted us to adopt two, why didn't He just tell us that in the beginning? We weren't ready to receive that call. That was too big of a step of faith for us at the time. We had two other families from our church who adopted two from the Congo and we thought they were crazy. God knew our hearts and how much faith we had at the time so He called us to a step. Once we opened our hearts to be obedient to that first step, our faith in God and our heart towards the orphan grew, so He called us to adopt another one.

You could explain it another way. Remember the principle: he who is faithful in little will also be faithful with much? Since we were faithful to be willing to adopt one, God was willing to entrust us with two. Anyone who has adopted can tell you the blessing we *receive* when we invite someone to join our family. God blessed us because of our obedience.

We should always be listening for God's voice. What percentage is God calling you to give *now*? Some of you heard clearly God's call on what you were to give a year ago. Or two years ago. Or five years ago. And you committed to obey back then and you have been faithful to this point. Is it possible that He is calling you to step it up now? Is it possible that He has been calling you to give more but you have not been listening for His voice?

As one of His investors, does God have access to His funds that you are managing? Did you give Him your cell number so-to-speak so that He can call night or day to request a withdrawal? Let's keep listening to God. If He is calling you to step it up, be obedient and trust that He will provide for your needs and bless your obedience. Just like it was an honor that God called us to adopt two, it is an honor that He invites us to do more for His kingdom!

I want to talk to those of you who are especially well off. Some of you make an amazing amount of money. God has blessed you with the brains and the work ethic and the opportunity to make money. If you make a lot of money, your heart is in a dangerous position. Since where your treasure is, there your heart will be also, then I would urge you to be careful. When you can afford so much more than the essentials, it is easier for your heart to be tethered. Think about this. If you give 10% (or less) to God, but spend 20 or 30% on an upgraded lifestyle, beyond your needs, where is your heart going to be pulled?

If we have money we can impact the lives of others. But if we love money we accomplish nothing. We don't have to serve money and stuff any more. We are called to experience something bigger. Why do you think that God gave you so much extra in the first place? I want to challenge you to step it up... a lot. There is so much you could do for the Kingdom of God.

I was reading recently that the IRS may be reducing the percentage of income that can be tax-deductible at 28 percent for couples whose incomes are at least $250,000. As of this writing, people can deduct 33%. Do you know why they are considering reducing it to 28% to create more tax revenue? Because there are so many couples who make over $250,000 per year that give more than 28% away that the government sees an opportunity to gain a huge increase in tax revenues. What if you sought to be one of those people who gave away that much or even more! Do you know what a difference $70,000 would make in your church's budget? Would you step it up and make it your goal to continue stepping it up in the future?

After the success of Rick Warren's *The Purpose Driven Life* which admittedly brought in millions and millions of dollars, Pastor Rick decided that rather than stepping up his standard of living, he increased his standard of giving and became a reverse tither. That means he started giving away 90% and only kept 10%. It would be easy to say that it is easy to live on 10% of millions, but I know that most people who make millions don't give away 90% of it, do they? It is an admirable thing to invest such an incredible percentage into eternal things.

If you began to live out these principles of The Generosity Revolution, what percentage could you live on in the future and just give the rest away? Wouldn't it be amazing to someday give away 50%? That would be the ultimate example of loving your neighbor as yourself, when you give away as much as you keep. Don't wait until God gives you more to be more generous. Give more now and watch God bless you so you can be more generous than you ever thought possible. Why not start increasing today? Why not step it up right now and set some radical generosity goals for the future and see what God does?

Heart Check

It may be easy for some of you to dismiss this chapter if you feel like you are already giving a significant amount to God's work. I can actually understand why people give a smaller percentage with the more money that they make. 10% or 15% or even 20% of the wealthiest income levels can seem like a big enough amount to give away. After all, it is so much higher than most people ever will do and can cover a significant ministry need. There is a story from Mark 12:41-44 I'd like you to read.

And Jesus sat down opposite the treasury, and began observing how the people were putting money into the treasury; and many rich people were putting in large sums. A poor widow came and put in two small copper coins, which amount to a cent. Calling His disciples to Him, He said to them, "Truly I say to you, this poor widow put in more than all the contributors to the treasury; for they all put in out of their surplus, but she, out of her poverty, put in all she owned, all she had to live on."

Either Jesus is really bad at math or there is something that we have been missing. It is not the amount of the gift that impresses God, but the amount of sacrifice that gift represents. All of these people who were giving large amounts, but small percentages of their income, did not impress Jesus at all. The gift by the widow caught the Lord's attention.

Has the level of sacrifice of one of your gifts ever done that? If our giving isn't really costing us, if it is coming out of our surplus, then maybe we need to raise it. If you are saying "we'll just" when you are giving, it may not be enough. It should not be easy. If your income is so high that you feel that giving 10% away is too big of an amount to give, then I would challenge you on that. If 10% is too high of an amount to invest in God's kingdom, then certainly 90% is too much for you to invest in yours.

Jesus said in Luke 16:13, "No servant can serve two masters; for either he will hate the one and love the other, or else he will be devoted to one and despise the other. You cannot serve God and wealth." The love of money and stuff occupies a space in many of our hearts as Americans that should only be occupied by Jesus. It is okay for us to have stuff, but for many of us, our stuff has us. If we can't serve both God and money how hard do you think Satan is working to try to get us to love money? If it is nearly impossible for a rich man to enter the kingdom of heaven, how hard do you think Satan is working to make us rich with stuff?

While we are in this story, I want to encourage those of you with smaller incomes too. I am sure that you may feel that your 1% or 2% would not make a difference since your income is so low. So why even bother? This woman put in virtually nothing, but it mattered deeply to God. It isn't always about what our gift can do in the world; sometimes it is simply about what our gift will do in us.

What do you think happened to that poor widow? Do you think she died of starvation that next week? I think God came through in a big way for her. I can't wait to meet her in heaven and hear how God met her need, how He blessed her for her step of faith. That has to be one great story. You can have a great story to tell also, but it is going to come after your step of faith.

Chapter Eleven

STEP IO

TRUST JESUS

One of the most comical statements in the Bible to me (and the Bible is full of them) is in Luke 1. Zacharias was a priest of the Lord and was chosen on this particular day to enter into the temple and burn incense as an act of worship. All of the people were gathered outside praying for him as he entered. We read that once inside, while he was all alone, the angel Gabriel appeared to him in all of his glory. I can't imagine what it would have felt like to see an angel. It is no wonder that the passage states that Zacharias was afraid.

The angel proceeded to tell him that even though he and his wife were well past the age of having children, they were going to have a son. Gabriel tells Zacharias that this promised child is going to be uniquely used by God as a forerunner to the Messiah. His son would grow up to be the one we know as John the Baptist. There is nothing comical about this scene yet, but the funny part comes in Zachariah's response. After hearing all of this explained by the angel, he responds with a question: "How can I be sure of this?" (Luke 1:18).

Really? How can you be sure? Think about it for a second, Zacharias. An angel is standing in front of you and is delivering this message. How can you be sure? You can be sure because of who it is who is making the statement. You can be sure that it will happen because of the one who is delivering the message.

I think sometimes we read statements in the Bible and think, "How can I be sure of this?" Here's one with which I am guessing you may struggle to believe. "It is more blessed to give than to receive" (Acts 20:35). Wow, really? We'll be happier, more fulfilled and satisfied, if we give more than if we get more? That is the opposite of everything the world and our flesh and the enemy tell us. Everything inside of us and everyone around us seems to be saying the opposite. You will be happier if you get more than if you give more. Don't we tend to neglect giving in order to pursue happiness in stuff? Is it really more blessed to give than to receive? How can we be sure of this?

Can I tell you how you and I can be sure of this? It is because of the one from whom the statement comes. Here's the entire verse: "In everything I did, I showed you that by this kind of hard work we must help the weak, remembering the words the Lord Jesus himself said: 'It is more blessed to give than to receive'" (Acts 20:35).

Jesus is the one who said we will be happier if we give more than if we get more. He says that this is true of me and that it is true of you. We still somehow scratch our heads as if to say, "Jesus can't be right, can He? Really?"

Yes, He really is right. We have got to trust Jesus if we are going to be a part of The Generosity Revolution. We need to believe both in the certainty of the reward of investing in eternity and that the reward of doing is better than consuming more on earth. You probably say you already do trust Jesus, but if we were honest, judging from the way we live our lives, most of us think Jesus was lying to us when he said this.

Look at your checkbook, your credit card statement, and your bank statements. That's how you will be able to tell if you really do trust Him. Jesus tells us what we are to do with our finances. Money comes with instructions, and He could not have been more clear on what our ultimate priority should be and the reason behind it. Look at Luke 12:33-34: "Sell your possessions and give to charity; make yourselves money belts which do not wear out, an unfailing treasure in heaven, where no thief comes near nor moth destroys. For where your treasure is, there your heart will be also." We are all aware that when we give the gift blesses the one who receives it, but that is not Jesus's point in this statement. He is not actually trying to motivate us by the need of the recipient. Whose happiness is Jesus concerned about when He is making this statement? The giver. Yours and mine as we give. He doesn't want us as the givers to miss out on the reward.

It takes faith to pass up spending money on yourself, doesn't it? To release it to God, and trust that you will be blessed in eternity as a result? But Jesus tells us to be investors in heaven, not earthly consumers.

He tells us that we will be rewarded. That we can actually store up treasures in heaven with our money now when we give it up to God. Not only that, but the reward we'll receive then is vastly superior to the rewards we can gain by spending. We will be blessed if we give. Andy Stanley tweeted, "Giving up something now for something better later is not a sacrifice. It is an investment." Do you have faith that the reward that is coming later, as a result our generosity, is better than what the reward would be now if we spent everything on us?

When we give to our churches and other ministries, eternities are impacted. But it is not just the eternity of those that we reach with those gifts, we, the giver, benefit from giving the gift for eternity. Think about that! God rewards us when we invest in His Kingdom. Jesus could meet every need that we come across by leading someone else to give, but Jesus wants you to enjoy the benefit. He invites you into the story. And if He's right, and I'm betting my money on Him, you will be more fulfilled now and happier for eternity. When you give to God, He sets aside rewards in your account in heaven. And when you get there, you will be so glad that you were generous during your time on earth.

I think I know what some of you are thinking right now. "Yeah, nice try. You just want my money. No way. Jesus is trying to trick me." Now you wouldn't say that out loud, but we show what we believe, not by what we say, but by what we do. I wonder if some of you in the back of your mind honestly believe that you might be disappointed if you lived a life of generosity. That you'll get the short end of the stick. Do you really think that Jesus is a con-artist? That you're going to get to heaven and see your inheritance after all of your sacrifice, all of your service to God, and be disappointed?

Do you think Jesus is duping you? Do you really think you are going to get to heaven and say, "I wish I would have driven a nicer car! Why did I round down and waste so much on God?" It is amazing how easily we get duped. We'll go buy a new car or boat or flat screen because we believe the commercial when it promises us happiness, but we won't believe Jesus when He tells us giving will bring eternal happiness. Is it even possible that when you get to heaven you are going to be disappointed that you didn't spend more on yourself while you were on the earth? Is there any way that you will regret any time you gave when you see the reward, your inheritance? I don't think so.

Jesus is not trying to trick you. He is trying to point you toward the best for you. He doesn't want you to regret your life, to waste the opportunity that you have. I saw a tweet a while back from Steven Furtick that said, "God doesn't want generosity from you. He wants generosity for you."

God doesn't need your money. He is not up there in heaven hoping that we'll give so He can do what He wants to do. God does not need any one of us to fund the work of His kingdom, but He has decided to use all of us. God delegated supplying for the temple to the people of Israel as we have already read in Malachi

3, and He has delegated the funding of His work in the world today to us. He does His work through the willing, voluntary, faithful sacrifice of His children, of those who believe that it is more blessed to give than to receive.

James tells us in Chapter 4 that our lives are but a vapor. Eternity is like a never-ending ocean in comparison. Why would we put our resources into the vapor? If you had some money to invest and you could only invest it in one of two companies, and one of those companies you knew was going in the toilet any day with no chance of coming out of it and the other showed a long run of promised growth, where would you put your money?

Jesus isn't lying to you. He wants what's best for you. Trust Him. He is not trying to trick you, and neither am I. Our kingdom, our time on earth will pass; it is temporary. Eternity is forever. We only have one life to invest during our short stay on the earth. Where are we going to invest it? In things that will fade away, or in that which will last forever? If we pursue money, maybe we will have 70 or 80 years, or even 90 to 100, to enjoy the rewards of what money can buy. But if we pursue Jesus and His purposes, we have an eternity to enjoy Him and the rewards that come with following Him.

The absolutely best thing we can do with the money entrusted to us is invest it in God's church and His work in the world. Why is that the best thing? Because when I keep extra money, it gets wasted on my pleasures, but when I give it, God uses it to change lives.

It is more blessed to give than to receive. There is no satisfaction that will come with the love of stuff. If you are not yet a follower of Jesus, I want you to understand that all of God's instruction about not loving money and about giving it away is not because He is trying to deprive you of pleasure; He is trying to save you from making your life about something that will disappoint. If money is your pursuit, you will never be satisfied. You are going to spend your life chasing after that which will leave you starved.

God invites you to seek your joy in Him. Why would God send His Son Jesus to die on a cross to pay for our sins and upon our belief in Him just sit back and let us chase things that would never satisfy? The more you get of Jesus, the more satisfied you are in Him. The more you get of anything else, the more you are dissatisfied with what you have. For those of us who have already placed our faith in God, He wants us to be satisfied and that can only come through Him.

God in His word says that the more you give, the happier you'll be. Society says the more you buy the happier you'll be. Who are you going to believe? Trust Jesus. Believe Him when He says that the rewards in heaven we will enjoy are directly proportionate to our generosity while we are on the earth. If we trust Him on how we can get to heaven, then let's trust Him on how to experience rewards in heaven.

One more thing on this topic. I don't believe that Jesus is just talking about being blessed in heaven. He is also saying that we will be blessed, more satisfied, here on earth as well. We all know people who are takers, right? They seem to only want to call when they have a need. They don't work hard themselves and expect others to cover for them. Are they happy? They always seem pretty miserable to me because they feel the world owes them, and they always feel like others are letting them down no matter how much others do.

What about the people you know that are most generous? They give of themselves, hold on to their possessions loosely, and practice hospitality with joy. Compare their level of fulfillment to the takers, those who only receive. There is no comparison is there. I've never met a miserable generous person. There is joy in giving. Our hearts are drawn toward others and to God when we give. After all, Jesus said that our hearts will follow where we put our treasure. Spending everything on ourselves increases our heart for ourselves, and we end up growing more selfish. There is no happiness there.

Both for now and for eternity, we really will be more blessed if we give more than if we receive more. We need to fight to believe that it is true. In spite of what the commercials says, in spite of what our eyes tell us when we see that shiny new car, and in spite of how the rest of the world seems to be living. Trust Jesus. Trust that Jesus really does understand money and our hearts and how the two work together, that He knows what will satisfy us. When we truly trust Him, we will spend like we believe Jesus and give like we believe Jesus. That is when we'll join The Generosity Revolution.

TRUST JESUS

Heart Check

Lack of faith in regards to what Jesus says about giving is one of those areas where so many of us have had it wrong for so long that we are genuinely afraid to even consider that we have been so far off course. It is as if we have been sailing on the open sea, heading a direction that we thought was taking us where we were supposed to end up, but now God has given us a glimpse of the horizon, and we can see we have been off course. What are you going to do now that you know? Just keep sailing and pretend that you don't know the truth? What are you afraid would happen if you changed course? I am praying that each of us who are confronted with this point or any other part of this book will not dismiss and continue as if it doesn't matter but will instead humbly come to our Father, admit we have wandered off course, and commit to following His intentions with our finances as we are called to in every area from today on. It does not matter how long we have journeyed the wrong direction and how much of His money we have squandered, we will find grace and forgiveness when we humble ourselves and come to Him with repentant heart.

In Luke 15, Jesus tells a parable of a son who asks for his portion of his inheritance while his father is still living and goes and wastes all of it on himself. What happens in the story when he humbles himself and returns to the father and acknowledges he was wrong?

He was accepted. He blew half of his father's wealth, but that didn't matter to the father. What mattered to the father was his relationship with his son. God can absorb the financial losses He has faced as a result of our wandering. He doesn't care about the money. He just wants a relationship with you, and "where treasure is, there your heart will be also."

CONCLUSION

I am sure that you have been challenged in this book and I trust that you have been inspired to join The Generosity Revolution. There is a story from the book of Haggai in the Old Testament with which I would like to end this book. I'll set up the context for you. The Jewish temple was destroyed nearly eighty-five years before the book of Haggai was written. Then about fifty years prior to its writing (thirty-five years after the temple was destroyed) a group of Israelites had returned to rebuild it. They finished the foundation, but after some threats and challenges they stopped working temporarily. They took a break... for fifty years! They forgot the very reason that they were sent back to Jerusalem in the first place and just ended up focusing on their own comforts. God confronted them through the prophet Haggai. *"Thus says the Lord of hosts, 'This people says, "The time has not come, even the time for the house of the Lord to be rebuilt" ' "* *(Haggai 1:2)*.

The people of Israel were basically saying, "It is okay that God's house is not in order, that it isn't built up. It is not an urgent issue." I'm sure they were planning to get around to it eventually. They just genuinely believed that there were other things that were more important, that took priority. They had been saying that for 50 years! They would walk by and see the temple lie there in ruins and somehow it didn't grab their heart. They had just come to accept it as okay.

Does it bother you that your church is under-funded or struggling to get by? Does it bother you that missionaries doing God's work around the world have to come back every three of four years to try to raise money again because so many supporters have dropped off? Does it bother you that so many kids are starving, young girls are trapped in the sex trade, and millions do not have clean water in the world? Too many of us are saying, "The time has not yet come to do something about these things" while we increase our own lifestyle with our extra.

God has something to say to them and to us. *"Then the word of the Lord came by Haggai the prophet, saying, 'Is it time for you yourselves to dwell in your paneled houses while this house lies desolate?'"* (Haggai 1:3). God says to them through the prophet, "Are you really okay with this? You guys are living it up. You've got your houses all taken care of. They are decked out with all the latest stuff. What about My house? What about the place where you gather to worship me? Where you learn about me and are filled spiritually?"

God calls them to straighten out their priorities and build His house.

"Thus says the Lord of hosts, 'Consider your ways! Go up to the mountains, bring wood and rebuild the temple, that I may be pleased with it and be glorified,' says the Lord. 'You

CONCLUSION

look for much, but behold, it comes to little; when you bring it home, I blow it away. Why?' declares the Lord of hosts, 'Because of My house which lies desolate, while each of you runs to his own house' " (Haggai 1:7-9).

I want to make sure we all understand that it wasn't that they didn't have resources or time to build His temple; it was that they had used everything that God gave them to build His temple on their own households. They were probably planning to give God the leftovers, but they just never seemed to have anything left over. There was always more to buy for themselves. Their priorities were backwards. Their lifestyles were requiring all of their resources and time. They were so wrapped up in their own lives that they neglected to give to the place where God's glory was proclaimed.

Is it possible that our priorities have been backwards? Is it possible that some of us have been so focused on building our house, that we have taken money and time that God gave us to give to Him and instead spent it on ourselves? I am not saying that God is not okay that we have nice houses or cars or other things if He gave us resources for those purposes, but is it possible that some of us spent more on our house than we were supposed to, that we diverted money that was supposed to be spent on God's house to pay for an upgraded lifestyle?

It is not that all other financial priorities are wrong; it is just that they are not the top priority. There are many great priorities. For example, paying off our house is a great goal. Getting out of debt is a great priority. I am a big fan of that. But that is not the first thing. It is not the biggest priority. Isn't it time for us to put Him first? Haven't we been building our own kingdom long enough? Haven't we invested enough into earthly things that will fade away?

I have always considered myself to be generous. In fact, I would have adamantly said that giving was the top priority in our household and had been for a long time. By the grace of God and some great teaching from my parents and others, we've always given first.

But there have been many times in the early history of The Pursuit when things have been tight financially, and I felt like I needed to take a paycut to try to help and have even had to give up a paycheck or two to make sure others on our team were able to get paid over the years. In addition to times when I have given up income, there have also been many times that we've given over and above what we had prayed about giving in order to help, not because I wanted to, but because I felt we had to. To be honest, many of these times it was frustrating to me. I put God first in my finances and was generally happy to give, but there were times that in order to give I had to pull money from my other priorities too, other line items in our spending plan, and that bothered me. Something clicked in me as I preached through this material a couple of years ago. I think I've had it backwards this whole time.

I wonder if a lot of us have had it backwards. We understand from the Bible that God is to be of first importance in our lives. You have probably heard that terminology used. When we talk about God being first in our lives, I'll tell you what it does not mean. It doesn't mean that He is just a little or even a lot higher above all our other priorities, as if He's the first line item in our priorities and then there is everything else that He has nothing with which to do. When we say God is first, it should mean that God is *over* but also *involved* in every priority in our lives. He is the center of everything. He impacts every area of our life when He is first. For example, God is above my wife and kids so I seek to be the type of husband and father He is calling me to be. God is above my work, so I am to work in the way He calls me to work in His word. We invite God to shape and disrupt any area of our lives with joy because of our love for Him, because He is first.

I have come to believe that God is calling us to allow giving to impact every area of our finances in this same way. I believe that is what it means to put God first in our finances, to surrender our finances to Him, to really be generous. "Giving" can and should be a line item in our budget, but true generosity can't just be that. What if generosity is supposed to be the priority around which everything else financially revolves, just like God is the priority around which everything revolves in our lives? What if it is supposed to be the center of our finances?

Giving is an action, being generous is a state of the heart. It is about priority. It is about what we seek first. What is the first thing you try to increase? What is the last thing you are willing do decrease? When expenses go up, where do you cut? When gas prices shot up the last time, did you pull money from giving to pay for it? If our hearts were with the kingdom of God, pulling from our giving would be the last place we would cut.

What do you hope to increase in the future, your eternal investment or just your earthly comforts? That may give you an indication of where your heart is. If we have a heart for earthly things, we give a certain amount to God and are excited that we get to spend the rest on what we really care about. If we have a heart for the Kingdom of God and our finances are centered on generosity, we spend less and less on earthly things and are excited that we get to give even more to what we really care about, which is the Kingdom of God. I think I've had it backwards at times.

What if the desire to be generous actually began to impact every area of our finances? What if before we made financial decisions, large or small, instead of asking if we could afford it, we asked, "How will this impact our ability to be generous, now and in the future?" I think that is what God wants from me. Maybe He is inviting you to live that way too. Haven't we lived with the wrong priority long enough? Haven't we placed our pleasures above God's kingdom for too long?

It is time for The Generosity Revolution. Where our treasure is, there our hearts will be also. We can't wait until everything is right in our personal lives to start investing in God's kingdom. There will always be more to buy. We can't focus just on our house and neglect God's anymore. We can't put our treasure primarily towards building our own kingdom and simultaneously have our hearts pulled towards God's. It does not work that way.

I hope and pray that you will become a part of The Generosity Revolution, not just for the sake of those who will be the recipients of your generosity, but for your own heart. I pray that as we put more of our resources into the Kingdom of God, our hearts will be irresistibly drawn towards Jesus until He becomes everything to us. Colossians 1:18 says this of Jesus our Lord: "He is also head of the body, the church; and He is the beginning, the firstborn from the dead, so that He Himself will come to have first place in everything." The time has come for us to put Him first in everything, including our finances. Welcome to The Generosity Revolution.

Appendix A

IS IT EVER OKAY TO SPEND

MONEY ON MYSELF?

Just like there are people who twist the Bible to justify their desire to pursue earthly riches, there are those who get the Bible twisted in their head and believe that all followers of Jesus are called to live in absolute poverty. "How can we allow ourselves to enjoy earthly pleasures when so many are suffering?" they might ask. I want you to clearly understand that this book is not preaching that we should never enjoy any of the money that God has entrusted to us.

I firmly believe that some of what God has put under our care, in fact for most of us the vast majority of it, is for us to provide for ourselves and our family's needs. Additionally, He gives us beyond what we need and allows us to enjoy some of His gifts too. We serve a generous God! James 1:17 reads, "Every good thing given and every perfect gift is from above, coming down from the Father of lights, with whom there is no variation or shifting shadow." God loves to splurge on His kids!

Although we are told that we must give up ownership of all of our possessions to God to become a follower of Jesus (Luke 14:33), the rich young ruler is told that he must sell everything and give it to the poor to have eternal life (Luke 18:22), and the apostle Paul lost all of his possessions and was still content (Philippians 4:11), the command for all Christians to live in poverty is not found in the Bible. The apostle Paul would have had the perfect opportunity to clarify that when he spoke to Timothy about how to guide those who had a lot of resources in the church where he pastored. But instead of telling them they should sell everything and live in poverty, look what Paul says in 1 Timothy 6:17-18:

"Instruct those who are rich in this present world not to be conceited or to fix their hope on the uncertainty of riches, but on God, who richly supplies us with all things to enjoy. Instruct them to do good, to be rich in good works, to be generous and ready to share, storing up for themselves the treasure of a good foundation for the future, so that they may take hold of that which is life indeed."

The passage clearly tells those of us who have a lot of resources to not to put our hope in our money instead of God. It instructs us to be ready to share in order to store up treasures in heaven. Paul wants us to make sure that we don't believe that life is found in possessions. He also says it is okay to receive from God, recognizing that God richly supplies us with all things to enjoy. God as our Father wants to give us gifts so that we can enjoy them.

Living on less can easily become an idol or something you feel is earning approval from God. Our acceptance by God is not determined by how much we give or how little we keep. Our approval comes from what Jesus did on the cross for us. God is already pleased with you. As a child of a generous Father, He has provided extra for us, just as we provide extra for our children. It brings joy to our Father when He blesses us by giving a gift. It is so easy to get caught up in generosity that we can begin to feel guilty as if we aren't doing enough because we still have money left over as a result of managing God's money well after we have given what we committed to give. Colossians 2:18 tells us, "Let no one keep defrauding you of your prize by delighting in self-abasement." The goal is not to be miserable. The goal is to be as generous as God has called us to be.

Suppose you wanted to give your child a gift so you gave them something special, but they had just heard of some other child in need so they said that they wanted to give it to them instead because they were content, you would probably praise that decision. You would celebrate their generosity. But what if *every* time you gave them a gift, birthday after birthday, Christmas after Christmas, they would never accept a gift from you? You'd probably wonder where you went wrong in your parenting, wouldn't you? There is something wrong if a child is never willing to accept a gift from their parents! Accept gifts from God! I used to really struggle in this area and am still working through it in my own life. I confess that I often struggle to spend money on myself or my family on things that we don't absolutely need, knowing there are other things we can do with that money that seem more urgent. We cannot let generosity become a duty if it was once a joy. The moment you start feeling guilty any time you spend money, that ought to be a red flag that you are forgetting that God is crazy about you and loves to see you smile.

I can remember a few years ago when we were forced to replace our vehicle because the one we had was totaled when a light pole jumped behind me at just the right moment, and I backed into it. We had previously set a limit in our home that we would never spend more than $10,000 for a vehicle and what we purchased had to be at least ten years old. We felt like that was a line in the sand that would significantly lower our automobile expenses over our lifetime.

Since I was a kid, I had always wanted a Toyota 4runner. (Isn't it interesting how our hearts are drawn to things far before we will even be able to really be able to use them?) We had $7500 to spend on a car since we were forced to buy something before we had intended (you know, the moving light pole!). We found a beautiful 12-year-old 4runner that was loaded. It had about 150K miles on it and was in our price range. Made perfect sense to get it, right? But I struggled. I was feeling guilty knowing that things were tight at our church and feeling like maybe we shouldn't have such a nice car. I honestly had to get encouragement from others and then talk myself into buying it.

Even when we owned it, I still would drive our older

mini van around because somehow I felt like God was happier with me if I was suffering. That, my friends, is warped. I had already spent the money. The 4runner was under our stewardship, a gift from God, something He wanted to give me because we had been faithful, and yet I felt guilty receiving it. I am not out of the woods yet, but I am learning that it is okay to enjoy the good gifts that God gives us. In fact, it is insulting if we refuse them. What if your spouse said "No thank you" when he or she unwrapped that perfect valentine's gift from you? Then let's not refuse the gifts from the Father. When we follow scriptural principles and establish a God-honoring spending plan and designate some of the money to be spent on ourselves, when the money is there, spend it! It is a gift from God.

You need to know your own limits and pay attention to your heart. If you continually practice generosity and begin to feel deprived unfairly, you need to examine your heart first as to why you give. What is your motivation? If your motivation is out of love as it should be, then perhaps you are giving more than you are actually called to give. Just as it is in our service to God, we need to have a sustainable pace of generosity, not push so hard that we burn out. There will likely be times that you will need to increase the amount on which you allow yourself to live and actually reduce the amount that you give away. There will be seasons where you feel called and have the ability to give more, but when those seasons pass, it is absolutely permissible to give less, and we do not have to feel guilty about doing so.

One final thought on this. If we want to be as generous as possible, remember to allow our spouses and children to be the recipients of that generosity too. I remember my dad sharing with me that his biggest regret with our family was that he did not spend enough time recreationally as a family. I never felt deprived, but that advice from a very godly man has encouraged me. Sometimes the best use of some of the extra will be to go on a cruise with your wife, take the family on a vacation or even just go out to dinner to celebrate your family. Family time is incredibly valuable and as our kids grow towards and into the teen years, using some of the money God has entrusted to us to foster good family time is important.

There is also a tremendous opportunity to bless others that are in your life who may not have the resources to enjoy some of the luxuries that you can afford. If your'e being generous and God has blessed you with the opportunity to own a personal watercraft or a four-wheeler or a vacation home even after you've given, that is a wonderful gift. You now have the opportunity to share those blessings with others who have not been blessed as richly as you have been. Be ready to share!

Give what God is calling you to give. If you aren't sure what that percentage is, ask Him, talk to your spouse, and get advice from some generous Christians you know. There is then freedom in your spending plan to enjoy some of the fruits of your labor. Even in that process of spending though, we can still use other principles we've discussed to make sure our hearts do not become tethered to these things we now are enjoying. We have the opportunity to round down and spend less than we would have spent when we were consumers so that we can be more generous in the future.

PARENTING AND THE

GENEROSITY REVOLUTION

"How do we teach our kids to be more generous?" is a question that should be a priority of parents who are a part of The Generosity Revolution. It is an important question because generous children grow up to be generous adults. If we don't capture their hearts early, it is going to be harder to make the shift later in life — and we know from experience that many never will make that shift.

Think back to your home life growing up. Was generosity promoted in your household? Did you grow up in a home where you were taught the importance of giving first, before you were allowed to spend? If you struggle with generosity now, there is a good chance that generosity was not taught as a main priority. I am not here to criticize how you were parented. Believe me, with five young children I am very aware of how we all fall short in different areas. Regardless of how you were parented, I want to challenge you to begin training your children in generosity even as they become toddlers.

Proverbs 22:6 says, "Train up a child in the way he should go, Even when he is old he will not depart from it." If we take the time to train up our children in generosity, when they grow up into adulthood, those lessons will stay with them. So let's start today, whatever the ages of your children.

With very young children, we start with the foundation of teaching them that everything is God's as I shared in Chapter 2. When your children begin to argue with other children over a toy, they will very soon argue their right to avoid sharing by pulling the "Mine" card. As soon as they start using this possessive word, as parents we need to step in and begin to guide their hearts. We need to graciously share with them that "their" toy is actually God's, and that He loans all of us things to enjoy them for ourselves but also to share. Start explaining this well before you think they will fully understand it. (It will be good to verbalize this as a reminder to you as well!) How will we expect our children to grow up to be adults that share if we do not instill that into their hearts as children? That is our responsibility as parents.

As your children begin to grow up and receive an allowance or wages for extra work that they perform around the home (whatever your philosophy), start them with a basic spending plan. You simply purchase three containers and label one "Give" one "Save" and the last one "Spend." Don't hand them a dollar bill when it is payday; give them change that they can divide up into the three jars. One mistake that I think many parents make who have used this approach is that they instruct their kids exactly what amounts to put in each jar. I think it is okay to give them guidance, but many times we as parents limit their generous hearts by telling them to give 10% and save 10%. "Here is a dollar. You have to put one dime in giving and one in saving and then you spend the rest." Our desire as parents should be that our kids grow up to be as generous as possible with the money God entrusts to them. Your kids will inevitably ask what they should do. Take the opportunity to encourage them to be as generous as possible and know that God will take care of them if they live that way.

When it comes to deciding what to give, we share with our children what we do if we receive money ourselves, and we share why — we trust God that He will take care of us. By the way, sharing what we would do is great accountability for ourselves as parents. I can understand why many Christian parents would not use this tactic. Since the average Christian gives 2.5% of their income toward charitable causes, they would not really want to pay their children a dollar in pennies and have them put two or three pennies in the giving jar! We need to cultivate generosity in our children, and in order to do that, we have got to live it ourselves before we can teach it.

When you see your children taking steps of generosity, we as parents have the ability to be God's provision for them. Not every time, but on occasion, we can reward them with something extra to show that God honors their generosity. Sometimes God will do it without our help. My daughter Meghan is incredibly generous as an 11 year old. A few weeks ago after school she found a $20 bill blowing across a parking lot. We celebrated the gift but also reminded her that God blesses those who are generous with extra. Remember, the promise that God will take care of those who practice generosity is not just for adults!

As far as savings, let them know that saving now means that they can spend it later. It is not money that is lost. They need to learn that to spend hastily often brings regret and limits our ability to purchase in the future. Many times our children will spend their money immediately on candy and then will ask us to purchase a toy that they want shortly thereafter. Buying them a toy at that point is a missed teaching opportunity. Instead we should explain to them that if they would not have spent all of their recent spending money immediately, they could have purchased the toy, but now they will have to wait. Help them establish savings goals and encourage them to save. It is important that you occasionally allow them to spend some of that money in savings if they have been faithful, otherwise saving can become discouraging. You can also occasionally add money to their savings and explain to them that when they are older and invest money, they will earn interest on it.

As your kids arrive into the elementary years, take the opportunity to teach your kids about rounding down. In our home, since we started very early talking about the importance of giving money to God, and we understand that if we spend it we can't give it, we needed to build this understanding into our children as well. When we go out to eat as a family at a sit down restaurant, our kids know that we all drink water with our meals instead of spending money on sodas, milk or juice. If it is not included with their kid's meal, they drink water. It is always the way we have spent when we have gone out to eat. We simply explain to them how much more it would cost if we paid for beverages, which would limit the amount of times we could go out to eat or rob us of the opportunity to be generous. Our kids have always agreed with us when we take the time to explain it, even though they really want soda

When we go to a fast food restaurant, we almost never get them a kid's meal. I want you to understand something: it is not the need or right of every child to get a kid's meal every time they go to a fast food restaurant. It is not abuse to round down It is smart. Help them understand that they don't need the milk with their meal. Why would we pay $1 for a tiny milk when you can buy a gallon for under $3? Take that milk container home with you one time and set it next to your gallon of milk. They can see that and will understand.

Our children know that we want to be generous as a family because we talk about it often, and by now they want it too. From the beginning we have helped them see that it isn't going to matter a few minutes later whether they got a kid's meal or not. They see very easily that if we all round down, we will have more available to give. Why not teach your kids to round down? In the same way, the idea of rounding down on movies and watching a DVD does not necessarily make sense to elementary children. They may see trailer on television for a movie and request that you see it right away. We need to help them understand. If it would cost your family $50 to go to a first-run theatre to see a movie, withdraw $50 in $1 bills from the bank and sit your children down and show them the stack of bills that it would cost to go see it right away, and then pull the stack away and leave just the $1 it would cost to see the movie at home on DVD and ask them which they think is wiser. If you do this when they are young, it will guide their choices in the teen years and even into adulthood. Children don't intuitively understand the other things that money could do if we don't spend it. If you can make it visible, using these types of illustration enough times early on, you will be cultivating an awareness and a habit of rounding down.

I spoke in Chapter Seven about paying for someone else's meal at the drive thru or leaving an extra-generous tip and leaving the recipient one of The Generosity Revolution cards. Our kids absolutely love doing this. I don't think you'll have to train your kids or talk them into wanting to participate in this act of generosity. When we first explained the idea, they were all for it. Every time we were driving somewhere, they wanted to "do The Generosity Revolution." Obviously this can add up pretty quickly. It is amazing how much some families spend at a fast food drive thru! (I wish everyone rounded down.) But once they desire to be generous in this way, we have the opportunity to talk to them about funding generosity with personal sacrifice.

At the appropriate time, we asked them if they wanted to do this regularly. All three shouted without hesitation, "Yes!" Kids can be so enthusiastic. But then we asked them how we were going to be able to continue to do it, explaining to them that the money has to come from some other category in our budget. It didn't take long for the oldest to say, "We will have to spend less going out to eat on us." They were all okay with that. They began to understand that the only way to be able to give more is to spend less on ourselves.

I can remember one time we were at a local sit down restaurant. We had received a text club invite to come in and enjoy free kids meals. We had some money left on a gift card, so our out-of-pocket expense for the meal was just over $4. We would have tipped off of the original total before the discounts anyways, but my Mallory, who was nine at the time, said she wanted to do The Generosity Revolution. I was thinking $20 when she said, "How about $100?" I asked her why, and she explained that she just really liked the server and she wanted to bless her.

We explained to her that we did not have room to do $100 since it was close to the end of the month, but if they were willing to not have any fun money to spend on ourselves for the rest of the month, we could do it.

All three kids thought about it and agreed that we should do this. I could not have been more proud of my kids who made a choice to spend less on themselves so that they could bless someone else. They really want to be a part of The Generosity Revolution! We have never left a restaurant so giddy. You should have seen the joy on our kids' faces. If we would have taken them to a really nice restaurant at their age, they would not have appreciated it or remembered it for any significant amount of time. But they will remember giving that tip for years. With all of the training we have done in the early years, I don't think there is any way they will grow up to just be consumers. The foundation is being laid.

As you start to practice generosity and they get a taste of what it feels like to give, you may discover that one or even all of your kids want to be generous with their money to the point where it makes you uncomfortable, feeling like they may be depriving themselves. What do you do? You may be tempted to step in and stop them, being unsure that they fully grasp what they are giving up to be generous, but we need to trust Jesus to bless our children too. If we believe that it is more blessed to give than to receive for us, then we can be confident that it is true for our children as well.

On the flip side, if we as adults have a hard time always sacrificing, we can be sure that our kids will have times there they struggle with the idea as well. It is in these moments that we can remind them of the faith to which we are called. I was recently in a department store with my two pre-teen daughters. They had been in the store ahead of me, looking for a particular item. When I walked over to where they were near the shoes,

Mallory, the younger one, said to me with urgency, "Dad, I need new shoes. The ones I have are falling apart." It really caught me off guard with her pleading tone. I reminded her that she had another pair that served her needs just fine. A few minutes later, she said in the same voice and tone, "Dad, I need new jeans. The only two pairs have holes in the knees." I told her that I wasn't aware of her need and we would look at them when we got home. A few minutes later, in the same tone and sense of urgency as her other two requests, she cried out, "Dad, I need new shorts." I was blown away. I told her that she did not need any new shorts. I could have just left it at that, but later that evening I was able to talk with her about greed, about the discontent that can happen in us if we are not careful. That we all hear voices telling us that we "don't have enough, that something new will satisfy us" and that she needs to learn to combat those voices with the truth, that we are blessed and have more than what we need. Don't miss the opportunity to address the heart issues behind statements when it comes to money. If our kids don't learn that from us, they will certainly be prone to consume beyond what they need when they have an income and can end up in the same debt situation where many in our generation have found themselves.

As they continue to grow older and face more choices, they will be challenged to stick with it when they see the rest of their friends going after the things of the world. How can we encourage them to stay focused? One key way is to share when God provides as a result of your generosity. It is one thing to say that He does, but our children need to see it happen. When you are the recipient of something good, verbalize that with your kids. Remind them that even though it is not your purpose to be a consumer, at times you are blessed. When you get a raise or you are the recipient of a gift card or anything else unexpected, share details with your children so they can see that God really does supply to those who are generous. As they begin to see that God delivers on His promises, they will be drawn to strive for generosity for themselves.

What kind of foundation are you establishing for your children? We are facing an uphill battle as our culture drives our children towards consumerism. Kids have a sense of entitlement these days. They feel like they are owed. Parents put pressure on themselves and continually have a desire to give their kids a "better" life than the one they received. Our kids have never asked us to provide a bigger house and nicer cars than I had in our home growing up. Have yours? Our kids don't know what we had! Why are we putting that kind of pressure on ourselves? Maybe our generation should be the first to step down in our amount of consumption. Perhaps we should take the time to look back on how we were raised and choose to actually live on less, to downgrade our standard of living.

If we believe that giving our kids a "better" life means enjoying more and more stuff and entertainment as a consumer, are we believing Jesus or believing the culture? If we believe Jesus and we want them to have a "better" life, we would be training them up to be radically generous people, not consumers. We are training up our children, whether we know it or not, where generosity falls on the priority list. Let's raise them up to be a part of The Generosity Revolution for the sake of those whose lives they can impact as they grow and for their own sake, believing that it is better to give than to receive.